Edward S. Herold

SEXUAL BEHAVIOUR OF CANADIAN YOUNG PEOPLE

Fitzhenry & Whiteside

To Malia

© Fitzhenry & Whiteside Limited 1984

Fitzhenry & Whiteside
195 Allstate Parkway
Markham, Ontario L3R 4T8

Canadian Cataloguing in Publication Data

Main entry under title:
Herold, Edward S. (Edward Stephen), 1943–
    Sexual behaviour of Canadian young people

Bibliography: p.
Includes index.
ISBN 0-88902-523-1

1. Youth – Canada – Sexual behaviour.   2. Young adults –
Canada – Sexual behavior.   3. Sexual ethics.   I. Title.
HQ27.H47 1984   306.7'088055   C84-098092-2

Printed and bound in Canada by John Deyell Company

Illustrations by Allison Dunlop and Penelope Moir.

Acknowledgements

The preparation of this book was made possible through the co-operation of several individuals and organizations. The most significant contributions were made by the following research assistants and graduate students: Marilyn Shirley Goodwin, Lynn Samson, Jane McNamee, Arlene Everets, Lori Wilson and Margo Stockie. Sincere appreciation is also expressed to Liz Chamberlain and Petra Zimmermann for carefully typing various drafts of the manuscript. I also wish to acknowledge the support given my research by my colleagues both within Family Studies at the University of Guelph and outside of this department. The following reviewed the manuscript and offered helpful suggestions: Dr. Richard Barham, Dr. Claude Guldner, Dr. Gordon Jessamine, Dr. John Lamont, Kelli-Ann Lawrance, Dave Massey, Joan Marsman, Gail Molloy, Lisa Pelletier and Shirley Wheatley.

Acknowledgement is given to the Family Planning Division, National Health and Welfare, Ottawa and the National Institute of Health, Washington, D.C. for the financial support these agencies have provided for my research.

Special thanks goes to my wife, Yvette for her emotional support throughout this project.

Contents

Introduction

In the 1950's parents were concerned about whether their teenagers should go steady with one partner. Today the major issue is whether teenagers should be provided contraception without parental consent.

Significant changes have occurred in the sexual attitudes and behaviour of Canadian youth since the early 1960's. These changes have been most notable for young women and currently about one-half of 19-year-old Canadian women have experienced premarital intercourse. Although pregnancy rates have levelled off, an increasing number of teenagers who become pregnant are opting for abortion. Of those who have children out-of-wedlock, most are keeping their babies rather than placing them for adoption.

Often simple explanations are given for these changes. Some believe that the pill by its removal of the fear of pregnancy has encouraged sexual permissiveness. Others blame the mass media for exploiting sexuality. The truth is that reasons for changing sexual behaviour are far more complex than these simple explanations.

Beginning in the late 1960's and continuing on into the 1970's, traditional authority was questioned and emphasis was placed on personal freedom and gratification. The ethic of instant gratification replaced that of deferred gratification and young people came to expect that they should be permitted to make their own decisions about matters such as sexuality. The changing norms affected women more than men as there was an increasing emphasis on the rights of women to determine their own lifestyles.

An underlying assumption of this book is that the most significant changes in sexuality have occurred among females and in order to understand changes in sexual behaviour we need to understand how the definition of female sexuality has changed. Today a common portrayal of woman is the enticing sexual being. Whereas in the past being sexually appealing was considered a negative trait and one to which nice girls did not aspire, the opposite is true now where "looking sexy" is considered a compliment.

Because of the many differing views and opinions expressed about premarital sexuality, there is a great deal of confusion and ignorance about the sexuality of young people. In this book I intend to dispel at least some of the confusion surrounding this topic through providing factual information based on contemporary research. In doing so I hope to provide a clearer picture of the major sexual issues and decisions facing Canadian young people. Some of the issues I will discuss are:

1. Have sexual attitudes and behaviour really changed?
2. Why do many sexually active teenagers not use contraception?
3. What are the main sexual concerns of young people today?
4. Is abortion used as a substitute for contraception?
5. What theories can help us understand premarital sexuality?
6. Why do some pregnant young women choose abortion while others choose to keep their baby?
7. How does adolescent parenthood affect the mother and her baby?
8. What role are parents playing in the development of their children's sexual standards?
9. How can we make our sex education programs more effective?

In answering these questions I am using insights acquired both as an educator and a researcher. I have taught human sexuality courses to university students since 1971. Through discussions with high school and university students, I have become aware of the powerful role that sex plays in the lives of young people and of the considerable anxieties, guilt and self-doubts many have about their sexuality. As a teacher of human sexuality, I am aware of the necessity to deal with attitudes as well as facts. Consequently, in this book I go beyond the presenting of statistics and provide a more complete understanding of the conflicting sexual pressures which young people are experiencing today.

Most of the information in this book is based on Canadian research including Statistics Canada data. On topics where Canadian research is lacking, studies from other countries, especially the United States, have been used to give more complete coverage of the subject.

Much of the material is based on my own research and that of my graduate students. Since 1971 I have conducted and supervised several studies on premarital sexuality, contraception and sex education. The major ones referred to in this book are surveys of university and community college students conducted in 1975 and 1982 and a survey of females attending birth control clinics in 1977.

In 1975 Dr. Roger Thomas and myself surveyed 481 single students at three universities and three community colleges in Ontario. We also surveyed 183 students from two high schools in Toronto. The study focussed on sexual and contraceptive attitudes and behaviours. In 1977 Marilyn Goodwin and myself surveyed 486 single females aged 13 to 20 who were attending 10 birth control centres in southern Ontario. The main objective was to determine factors influencing contraceptive use. In 1982 Leslie Way, Dorothy Kitchen and myself surveyed 363 students at the University of Guelph. Dorothy Kitchen focussed on the sexual and contraceptive attitudes and behaviours of males and Leslie Way and I analyzed data on female sexuality including self-disclosure and non-coital sexual behaviour.

In addition to these main studies I have also supervised studies of sexual assault, sexual fantasies, adolescent fathers, mother-daughter communication about sex and the teaching of sex education in the schools.

This book is designed for courses in which the sexual behaviour of Canadian young people is a major topic. The information will also be useful to professionals who educate or counsel young people about sexual issues. This includes teachers, physicians, nurses, social workers and clergy.

The book will be of direct value to young people themselves. In university sexuality courses, I have found that students prefer a frank and open presentation of factual information so that they can obtain a clearer understanding into their own sexual development. I have used that approach in this book in trying to deal with the concerns young people have about their sexuality. So that young people will find the material more personally relevant I have included numerous case history examples. These examples not only make the academic material more interesting, but they help students to relate to the information on a more personal level.

I also hope that parents will read this book and become more knowledgeable about the sexuality of young people. Hopefully, this will encourage parents to communicate more effectively with their own children about this important dimension of life.

Canadian Attitudes to Premarital Sex

As a Christian I believe that intercourse is for marriage.

At age 15 I believed: "I'll never have sex until marriage." At age 18 I believed: "If you are in love then sex is okay." At age 21 I believe: "If you are both in the mood, then why not."

I am not concerned if other people are labelling me as promiscuous because I want to be free to do what I want to do. I wouldn't associate with people who would say things like that.

My teacher stressed that girls should not fool around with boys as boys could be aroused very easily and have the urge to go all the way. Sex was different for the male than for the female. It seemed that the girl was always blamed for seducing or letting the boy go all the way whereas the boy was excused for his behaviour as sex is a natural need. Sex for males involved pleasure; the female was used to satisfy his pleasure.

These remarks made by Canadian youth illustrate the considerable differences of opinion regarding premarital sex.

It should be noted that the term premarital sex is used in this book to refer to sexual intercourse among young single people.

Societies vary greatly in their attitudes toward premarital sex. In a study of primitive societies, George Murdock (1949) found 70% accepting of premarital coitus. In contrast, the Moslem societies emphasize female chastity and consider it the most precious possession a woman can bring to a marriage. In some instances the husband on his wedding night is expected to show his relatives the blood-stained sheet of the wedding bed to demonstrate the purity of his wife. In Iran one man reportedly killed his twenty-three-year-old sister after discovering she was pregnant. She claimed to have had sexual relations with an American embassy hostage. The man justified the killing by saying that he did it in order to save family honour (The Globe and Mail, April 1, 1980). In Iran it is a crime to have sexual relations with an unmarried woman and conviction can lead to ten years imprisonment. In some Moslem countries there is such an emphasis on controlling female sexuality that girls have their clitoris surgically removed prior to puberty. These societies believe female circumcision reduces a woman's sexual drive and helps to protect her chastity.

In Japan virginity at marriage has traditionally been considered so essential that young women who lost their virginity would sometimes request surgery to mend the hymen. This was originally begun to assist rape victims who found it difficult to marry after the rape because of the loss of their virginity. However, with increasing sexual permissiveness, the demand for mending the hymen by plastic surgery has decreased.

Until recently most Western societies were opposed to premarital sex. Of the Western nations, Sweden was among the first to accept a permissive set of sexual norms for young people. The fact that organized religion has relatively little influence in Sweden and only a small percentage of Swedes attend church may account for this permissiveness. Also the Swedes have had a tradition of accepting premarital sexual relations when a couple was involved in a committed relationship prior to marriage.

Swedish acceptance of premarital sex is reflected in the term used to describe first intercourse. In Canada we use the negative expression of "losing one's virginity" whereas Swedes refer to one's "sexual debut". In Sweden there is no generation gap over sexual values because most parents expect their adolescent sons and daughters will engage in sexual relations. Because of this acceptance, Swedish parents are more likely than Canadian parents to discuss contraception with their teenage sons and daughters. Sweden was the first country to make sex education compulsory in the school system. Although Swedes approve of premarital sex in a love relationship they generally do not approve of casual sexual relations. Also the Swedes, because they emphasize the commitment aspect of a relationship, are generally opposed to extramarital relations (Moskin, 1971).

Canadian Attitudes

Do Canadians approve or disapprove of premarital sex? There are many ways to approach this question. The most scientific is to take a random sampling of people and ask them. This was done by the Gallup Poll survey organization in 1970 and 1975. Canadians were asked "Do you think it is wrong for a man and a woman to have sex relations before marriage or not?" The surveys showed Canadians divided on this issue with no clearcut acceptance or rejection of premarital sex. However, in 1975 there was a change toward greater acceptance of premarital sex with fewer than one-half of Canadians saying they did not disapprove of premarital sex and 17% undecided (Toronto Star, March 29, 1975). Men expressed a more accepting view than did women. Younger Canadians were the most accepting with 70% of those under age 30 approving of premarital sex compared with 27% of those age 50 and over. Favourable attitudes toward premarital sex were also held by those having a university education or higher income. Parents with teenagers living at home were far less accepting of premarital sex than parents not having teenagers living at home.

Further evidence of a trend toward acceptance of premarital sex is given in a 1977 survey of Weekend Magazine. The Weekend Magazine poll asked 1061 Canadians in 32 urban centres their opinion on premarital sexual behaviour for single adults. In total, 58% were approving and 24% were disapproving with the rest undecided (Weekend Magazine, Dec. 3, 1977).

In August 1979 the Gallup Poll organization, on behalf of the Toronto Star, conducted a random telephone survey of 427 adults living in Toronto. Seventy-one percent said that sex before marriage was acceptable for a man and 62% said it was acceptable for a woman.

The majority were also in favour of unmarried couples living together, with 69% of the men and 55% of the women agreeing that unmarried couples could live together. The survey also indicated a trend toward greater equality in sexual relationships for men and women, as only 25% said that sex was more important to a man than to a woman. The 1979 survey reflects the belief that women as well as men have sexual needs and suggests that sex is as important to women as it is to men.

A more recent national survey conducted by University of Lethbridge sociologist Reginald Bibby in 1982, suggests a further increase in acceptance of premarital sex as 74% of Canadians indicated that premarital sex is "not wrong at all" or wrong only "sometimes". This was an increase from 68% in a similar survey done by Bibby in 1975. Approval varied little between men and women but was much higher among the under 30 age group.

These changes in sexual attitudes were part of other fundamental personal and societal changes occurring during the late 1960's and 1970's. During this period, traditional values in almost all areas of life were questioned and replaced by values emphasizing individual freedom and personal growth. There was a trend toward the ethic of living for the moment, as instant gratification replaced deferred gratification and concern for traditional respectability.

Religious Attitudes

Until the early 1960's premarital sex was universally condemned by organized religious groups in North America. However, during the 1970's the religious perspective of premarital sex as sinful was questioned. Within many religious groups there was a debate between those following the standard of traditional religious morality and those proposing a new morality of situational ethics. In 1977 a committee of the Catholic Theological Society of America issued a study "Human Sexuality: New Directions in American and Catholic Thought" in which the morality of premarital sex was judged on the basis of whether the behaviour contributed to personal wholeness and growth rather than on the basis of traditional absolute do's and don'ts about sex. The report was denounced by the National Conference of Bishops which stated that the study conclusions "were not safe for people to follow". Opposition to the report was reinforced by Pope John Paul II who has been adamant about the sinfulness of premarital sex.

Similar debates took place within some of the Protestant denominations. In 1980 a Canadian United Church task force on human sexuality chaired by Rev. Robin Smith recommended that the church should not dictate whether premarital sex was right or wrong but should leave it up to individuals to decide for themselves.

On the other hand, among the conservative Protestant denominations the view of premarital sex as a sin continued to be a non-debatable issue. Ezra Taft Benson, head of the Mormon Council of the Twelve Apostles, in counselling the youth of his church to live morally clean lives, stated:

> *The world may countenance premarital sex experiences, but the Lord and his church condemn in no uncertain terms any and every sex relationship outside of marriage . . . Among the most common sexual sins are necking and petting which often lead to fornication, pregnancy and abortions.*
>
> Honolulu Star Bulletin, 1978

Similar sentiments were expressed by psychiatrist Dr. M.O. Vincent (1971) in his book *God, Sex and You* in which he criticized theologians for being reluctant to say whether premarital sex is right or wrong. According to Vincent, the Bible is clear in placing sexual intercourse within the bounds of a loving marital relationship. Thus, Vincent concludes the new morality is a distortion of Christianity.

However, the most serious challenge to traditional views of sexual morality has been the tendency of the laity to question the right of religion to dictate one's personal sexual morality. A powerful example of this is the rejection by many Catholic women of their church's position on the use of artificial means of birth control. Among sexually active young Catholic university women there is practically no difference from Protestant women in the use of mechanical means of birth control such as the pill (Pool & Pool, 1978). With a national sample of Canadian women Badgley et al. (1977) found little difference between the proportion of Catholics and Protestants using contraception with 81% of the Catholic women and 83% of the Protestant women using contraceptive means.

The Mass Media

Many people attribute increased sexual permissiveness to the influence of the mass media. Advertisers are accused of presenting sexy models and situations for the purposes of manipulating sexual appetites. While the media may have some impact on values, they are also a barometer of society in that they generally reflect rather than lead public opinion. It can be difficult if not impossible for the mass media to present ideas which are not accepted by most of society. For example, in the early 1960's Canadian author Pierre Berton received considerable criticism because he wrote an article in Maclean's magazine stating if his daughter were to have premarital sex he preferred she did it in a bed rather than in the back seat of a car. At that time many people considered his suggestion to be outrageous and flooded Maclean's magazine with complaints. If Mr. Berton were to write a similar article today, it is unlikely this would arouse as great a controversy as it did in the early 1960's. This incident illustrates how media are limited in the extent to which they can present viewpoints too divergent from the mainstream of society.

Another indication of how the media are dependent upon societal attitudes is seen in the romance novels written for women. Until the late 1970's the Harlequin Romance novels dominated the market. However, by the early 1980's publishing competitors were taking readers away from Harlequin. A major feature these other books offered was more sexual explicitness than found in the Harlequin books. For many years Harlequin Romances had been written with the premise that women wanted to read romance stories which omitted sexual scenes. However, with declining readership, this premise was called into question and Harlequin editors had to consider offering more "realistic" stories for the modern woman.

Although the impact of the mass media on sexual mores is debatable, there can be no doubt that media portrayal of sexuality has changed. Instead of presenting sex as bad and dirty, the media has been saying that sex is fun and exciting. In the 1970's nudity and explicit sex became commonplace in films. It was no longer shocking to hear people reveal personal details of their sexual lives in a public broadcast. Instead of exalting the innocent virgin, the media emphasized the sexually aggressive woman who not only liked sex but admitted it. A classic example is the 1977 film "Looking for Mr. Goodbar" which portrayed a woman almost totally consumed by her desire for sexual pleasure. In 1980 the film "Little Darlings" featured Kristy McNichol and Tatum O'Neal as two young teenage girls competing to see who could lose their virginity first. Although these films showed women having sexual freedom, this freedom was often tempered by portraying sexually-free women as being unhappy or suffering negative consequences.

In 1982 the film "Porky's" presented a humorous portrayal of teenage boys and their search for sexual adventure. In 1983 pay TV came into Canadian homes with an offering of "adult" movies and Playboy entertainment. Also, in the 1980's sexually explicit firms on videotape became more available with the introduction of video recorders into many homes.

A countervailing force was the National Film Board film "Not A Love Story" which attacked pornography and the sexual exploitation of women. This film was instrumental in sparking many women's groups to protest sexually degrading portrayals of women in the media.

Magazines have also been presenting a changed image of sexuality. To determine how the portrayal of premarital sex had changed, we compared mass circulation magazines of 1963 with those of 1973 (Herold & Foster, 1975). The magazines analyzed were Reader's Digest, McCall's, Ladies Home Journal, Good Housekeeping, Time and Chatelaine. In 1963 articles about teenagers focused more on dating than on premarital sex and there was considerable discussion over steady dating because of fear this might lead to premarital sex. None of these magazines suggested that it might be appropriate to provide birth control to sexually active teenagers, rather the emphasis was on maintaining traditional morality. On the other hand, in 1973, some articles questioned the traditional sexual morality. For example, the following statement was in Good Housekeeping, January 1973:

> *The rightness or wrongness of sexual intercourse is determined not by the legality of the relationship but by its quality.*

An article in the May 1973 Chatelaine magazine took an even stronger view:

> *The end of virginity as a value is part of the demise of the view of women as possessions instead of people—like pots fresh from the factory in which no one's yet baked. I've never been sure what men thought they were getting when gifted with someone's virginity, but I doubt that many of them will miss the awkwardness, self-righteousness and self-obsession that went with it as well.*

Complementing this shift in attitude was the discussion of contraception rather than abstinence as the answer to teenage pregnancy:

> *For years, says Dr. Cutright, "we have tried to use fear of pregnancy as a deterrent to premarital intercourse, and it hasn't worked. It's time to try something else." Dr. Cutright feels that the humane and reasonable alternative is birth control for minors.*
>
> (Ladies Home Journal, February, 1973)

Helen Gurley Brown in her book *Sex and the Single Girl* created a sensation in the 1960's by suggesting that single women could be sexual. A major spinoff from her book was Cosmopolitan magazine with its continuous record of exalting the sexuality of the single woman.

Similarly, for single males, Hugh Hefner through Playboy magazine emphasized the "new morality" and the benefits of recreational sex.

In the 1970's there were many women writers who focused on female sexuality. One of the most notable was Xaviera Hollander who, beginning with the book *The Happy Hooker*, presented the message that women could be sexual without penalty and that women should be free to search for sexual fulfillment in whatever manner they wished. Xaviera was granted celebrity status and was a sought-after speaker by the media and college campuses.

In terms of changes in public entertainment for women, certainly the most revolutionary was the introduction of the male stripper during the 1980's. Women across Canada went by the thousands to yell and cheer as they watched men disrobe on stage. Some women even hired strippers to perform at charity fund raising events. This one change clearly demonstrated that women's sexual attitudes were changing and that they could view men as sex objects.

Expert Opinion

Prior to the 1960's most professional experts such as psychologists and psychiatrists were opposed to premarital sexual activity for adolescents and claimed that premarital sex would inevitably lead to negative physical and psychological consequences. During the 1960's and continuing into the 1970's an increasing number of experts began to publicly state that premarital sex is not necessarily harmful. The psychologist Albert Ellis (1963) declared that sex should be seen as fun rather than as forbidden and that premarital intercourse should be accepted for well-adjusted persons. Lester Kirkendall (1961), a sociologist, proposed that premarital intercourse was not good or bad in itself but should be judged by its effects on interpersonal relationships. Warren Gadpaille (1975), a child psychiatrist, pointed to societies where premarital sex is accepted and where adolescents do not seem to be harmed by engaging in it. Dr. Diane Sacks, a pediatrician in the adolescent clinic at Toronto's Hospital for Sick Children, said she is *not* convinced "these kids, medically or physically, are going to be any worse for having sex at 14, if they're ready" (Maclean's, March 31, 1980). Yet other experts such as psychiatrist M.O. Vincent remained adamantly opposed to premarital sex and firm in their belief that premarital sex results in exploitation and other problems.

The writer Eleanor Hamilton (1978), while accepting premarital intercourse for older teenagers, contends that younger teenagers are not ready for the implications, such as pregnancy, that having intercourse involves. Hamilton (1978) strongly urges teenagers to consider non-coital sex as an alternative means of sexual expression. She gives explicit instructions on how couples can sexually excite each other through petting to orgasm which she claims could be just as satisfying as intercourse.

One noteworthy opinion leader is Ann Landers whose newspaper advice column is read by millions of people. Until the early 1970's Ann Landers disapproved of premarital sex and said the best birth control device was for a woman to keep her legs crossed. However, around the mid 1970's she began to modify her views. While still disapproving of premarital sex, she was in favour of providing contraception to teenagers because she believed that "once they have begun to experience sex they will probably do so again." She added:

This is not being permissive, it is just common sense. I say it is far better to permit sexually active young people to buy protection than to deny it to them and let them (and us) suffer the consequences.

(Guelph Daily Mercury, December, 1976)

Premarital Sexual Intercourse: What's Happening?

Sexual Attitudes of Young People

What are the attitudes of Canadian young people toward premarital sex? Today few young people believe they need a marriage commitment to have intercourse. This is a significant change from the 1960's when most believed intercourse was not acceptable until one was at least engaged. Among both sexes the standard of permissiveness in a love relationship has replaced the standard of sexual abstinence. In our study of high school and university students, 80% of males and 74% of females said premarital intercourse was acceptable if they felt strong affection for their partner (Herold & Thomas, 1978). There were significant differences between the sexes in attitudes about casual sex with only 6% of women but 42% of men agreeing that premarital intercourse would be acceptable to them even if they did not feel affectionate toward their partner.

In a study of high school students in Calgary about 80% believed that intercourse was acceptable if the couple were in love (Meikle et al., 1981). There were hardly any differences between males and females for this attitude. However, the males were more accepting of casual sex.

For most women being in a love relationship is a prerequisite to engaging in premarital intercourse. Women have been conditioned to associate love with sex and are less willing than men to engage in sexual relations solely for obtaining physical pleasure. Also, if women are in a love relationship, there is less chance of their partner exploiting or gossiping about them and this gives protection against acquiring a "loose" reputation.

However, not all students are accepting of premarital intercourse, especially those who are religious. In our research among females who attended religious services once a week or more, fewer than one-half (41%) accepted premarital intercourse with affection; whereas, among those who never or rarely attended church almost all (86%) were accepting of premarital intercourse. Religious males were also less accepting of intercourse with affection but not to the same extent as females. Among males who attended church once a week or more 63% were accepting of intercourse with affection compared with 87% of those who never or rarely attended.

Changes in sexual attitudes have produced a new definition of promiscuity. In the 1960's a woman who engaged in premarital sex was considered promiscuous. Today a promiscuous woman is more likely defined as one who engages in casual sexual encounters with many partners. There is still a negative label attached to the woman who has many sex partners and young women still worry about acquiring a "loose" reputation and possibly being labeled a "slut". Many males feel uncomfortable with a young woman who has had many partners and believe that she is "cheap" and "easy". On the other hand, for the male who has many sexual partners there is the positive connotation that he is a "real" man or a "stud".

As sex with affection has become a commonly accepted standard among young people, the idea of equating premarital sex with sin has diminished. In the 1950's and early 60's loss of virginity was seen as loss of purity and innocence. Today, one's reputation is less equated with loss of virginity. Actually the pendulum has swung as far toward the acceptance of permissiveness that some young people who have not experienced intercourse may feel there is something wrong with them.

Another consequence of changing sexual attitudes is that male expectations regarding sexual behaviour in a dating situation have changed. In the 1950's a girl could say no to a dating partner with the explanation that "if you truly love me, you wouldn't ask to do this". Today the situation has been reversed so that many males believe "if you truly love me then you will have sex with me."

Many adults view this changing sexual permissiveness with alarm and believe changing moral values will inevitably lead to society's decay. Some equate current sexual attitudes with the decadent time period prior to the fall of the Roman Empire.

Differences in attitudes between young people and adults are often referred to as the generation gap. We asked students what the reaction of their parents would be if they found out the students were having intercourse. Almost all females (86%) and most males (68%) said their parents would be upset. In contrast, only one-third of females and 13% of males said their friends would be upset to find this out.

Premarital Sexual Intercourse

Has sexual behaviour really changed? North American studies in the early 1960's found little change in sexual behaviour over the previous years. However, in the late 1960's researchers were beginning to report significant increases in the rates of premarital intercourse, particularly among women. In the 1970's these rates further increased. In the United States the best known surveys of adolescents have been done by Zelnik and Kantner of Johns Hopkins University who interviewed random samples of never-married females aged 15-19 in 1971 and 1976. During that five-year period the percentage of sexually active young women increased from 15% to 18% among 15-year-olds and from 47% to 55% among 19-year-olds. Also the age at first intercourse had dropped from 16.5 in 1971 to 16.2 in 1976 (Zelnik & Kantner, 1977).

Although most Canadian studies have been done with high school or university students, there has been some research with young people outside of the high school or university setting. In 1971 University of Quebec sexologists Crepault and Gemme (1975) surveyed

TABLE 1
CANADIAN SURVEYS OF PREMARITAL SEX
AMONG UNIVERSITY STUDENTS

Researcher	Sample Size	University Location	Date	% Experienced Intercourse	
				Males	Females
Mann (1967)	120	Ontario, Western	1965	35	15
Barrett (1980b)	415	Ontario, U. of Toronto	1968	40	32
Hobart (1972)	1,104	Alberta, Ontario, Quebec	1968	56	44
Mann (1969)	153	Ontario, York	1969	51	31
Perlman (1973)	156	Manitoba	1970	55	37
Perlman (1978)	259	Manitoba	1975	62	45
Pool & Pool (1978)	404	Ontario, Carleton	1975	—	66
Pool & Pool (1978)	390	Ontario, U. of Ottawa	1975	—	53
Herold & Thomas (1978)	481	Ontario	1975	64	55
Hobart (1979)	2,062	Five provinces	1977	73	63
Barrett (1980b)	1,384	Ontario, U. of Toronto	1978	62	58
Herold, Way, & Kitchen	363	Ontario, Guelph	1982	60	52

a random sample of young single adults aged 19 to 22 in Montreal and found that 60% of the males and 45% of the females had experienced intercourse. Ten years later in 1981 Dr. J. Frappier, Director of Adolescent Medicine at the University of Montreal, surveyed 140 students at a community college in suburban Montreal. The students had a mean age of 18.7 and thus were younger than in the earlier Montreal study. Frappier found that 55% of the males and 53% of the females had experienced sexual intercourse. In Saskatchewan a survey of 15 to 19 year olds was conducted in 1979 and 1980 by the Saskatchewan Ministry of Health (Weston, 1980). Thirty-five percent of the 15 to 17 year olds and 61% of the 18 and 19 year olds indicated they had experienced intercourse.

Since 1974 studies have been done with samples of high school students in Canada.

—*In 1974 University of Guelph psychologist John Hundleby (1979) surveyed grade 9 and 10 students in Ontario schools. Of the grade 9 students, 22% of the boys and 15% of the girls had experienced intercourse. Of the grade 10 students, 33% of the boys and 25% of the girls had experienced intercourse.*

—*Also, in 1974, high school students were surveyed at five schools in London, Ontario (Stennett et al., 1975). About one-third of the grade 11 students and 53% of the grade 13 males and 39% of the grade 13 females had experienced sexual intercourse.*

—In 1975 I surveyed grade 12 and 13 students in two Toronto high schools and found that 57% of the males and 33% of the females had experienced intercourse.

—In a survey of Calgary schools in 1980, 24% of the 14 year-olds and two-thirds of the 18 year-old males and females reported having experienced intercourse (Meikle et al., 1981). Only a slightly higher percentage of males than of females reported having experienced intercourse.

These results clearly indicate that a significant proportion of older adolescents are experiencing sexual intercourse. At the same time we should also recognize that most younger adolescents are not experiencing intercourse.

Several surveys have been done of university students. The first recorded Canadian study of premarital sex was by W.E. Mann (1967) at the University of Western Ontario in the mid 1960's. When Mann conducted his study there was considerable debate about whether premarital sex was an acceptable topic for research. However, by the 1970's research on premarital sex had become acceptable both in the social scientific research community and to the general population. Mann found that 15% of the females and 35% of the males surveyed had experienced premarital intercourse. More than ten years later Charles Hobart (1979), studying university students in five Canadian provinces, found that 73% of the males and 63% of the females had experienced intercourse. The most dramatic change was for females, who were approaching males in terms of sexual experience.

Data from the university surveys clearly indicate that more than one-half of university students have experienced premarital intercourse (see Table 1). The percentages also indicate that since the middle 1960's and early 1970's there has been an increase in the proportion experiencing premarital intercourse. However, the proportion who are sexually experienced seems to have stabilized since the middle 1970's.

In 1975, Dr. Roger Thomas and myself surveyed 481 students at three universities and three community colleges in Ontario. In 1982 graduate students Leslie Way, Dorothy Kitchen and I surveyed 363 students at the University of Guelph. In each survey the students were primarily in their first year. We found that the proportion of students having experienced intercourse was basically unchanged from 1975 to 1982. In our 1975 survey, 64% of the males and 55% of the females had experienced intercourse while in 1982 the respective percentages were 60% and 52%. The slightly lower percentages in 1982 could be attributed to the fact that this sample was slightly younger than the 1975 sample. Also, the 1975 sample was from only one of the universities studied in 1975.

The number of sexual partners was about the same in 1982 as in 1975. Among the sexually experienced university females in 1975, 47% had intercourse with one partner and 19% had four or more partners, while in 1982, the respective percentages were 53% and 19%. Among the sexually experienced university males, in 1975, 32% had intercourse with one sexual partner and 25% had more than four partners, while in 1982, the respective percentages were 36% and 32%.

It should be noted that the proportion who are sexually experienced is much higher among the older age groups. Research findings with university students usually are based on samples from first or second year courses. Because the percentage of young people experiencing intercourse increases with age, the fact that much of the research is based on the younger student population means that the percentage of young people given as having experienced intercourse before marriage is underestimated. For example, in our research of the single 21 year-olds, 80% of the males and 74% of the females had experienced intercourse.

The sexuality of those who have intercourse at an early age differs considerably from those who experience intercourse later. Tavris and Sadd (1975) found that women who have intercourse at younger ages are more experimental regarding sex in their later years. They have more premarital partners, masturbate more often, are more likely to combine sex with marijuana and more likely to have extramarital intercourse after marriage. They are also more likely to have homosexual experiences. In summary, those who have sex at younger ages are likely to place a greater emphasis on the importance of sexual gratification, and are willing to experiment with different ways of achieving this gratification.

In our research we also found that those who experienced intercourse at an early age had a greater number of sexual partners. Among males who experienced intercourse before the age of 16, 17% had one sexual partner and 40% had 6 or more, whereas among males who first had intercourse at age 18 or later 63% had one sexual partner and 7% had 6 or more. Among females, of those who first had intercourse before the age of 16 only 9% had one sexual partner and 34% had 6 or more. In comparison, 66% of females who had first intercourse at age 18 or later had one partner and only two percent had 6 or more.

Those who have intercourse at younger ages are more likely to tell their parents about their sexual activity. This is particularly true for women. Thirty-nine percent of the females who had intercourse before the age of 16 had told their parents about having intercourse compared with only six percent who began intercourse at age 18 or later. Among the males, 22% of those who had had intercourse before age 16 had told their parents compared with 17% who began intercourse at age 18 or later.

Most of the sexually experienced (85% of the females and 76% of the males) had told their friends about having experienced intercourse. Thirty-two percent of the males and 28% of the females had told four or more friends. Given the fact that most friends feel positive about premarital sex, it is not surprising that most young people are willing to share this information. This is a contrast from the 1960's when women especially were less likely to tell others because of peer disapproval of premarital sex.

One way in which sexual relations have not changed is that it is still largely the female's responsibility to act as a gatekeeper or to set limits on sexual activity. In a study of college students Peplau et al. (1977) wanted to find out what factors determined if intercourse would occur in a dating relationship. When both partners began the dating relationship as virgins, one-half of the couples had intercourse. When both partners had previous sexual experience all of them engaged in intercourse in their current relationship. What is most interesting was the situation where one person was experienced and the other was not. In this case the woman's experience was a stronger predictor of the couple's sexual behaviour than the man's. In every case where a male dated a partner who was sexually experienced that couple engaged in intercourse. In contrast, where a virginal woman dated an experienced male, one-third of the couples abstained. The researchers also found that the timing of first intercourse, or in other words, how early in the dating relationship intercourse occurred, depended primarily on the past sexual experience of the woman rather than of the man. If the woman was sexually experienced the couple had intercourse within an average of two months regardless of the man's experience. Thus despite more permissive attitudes, women are still expected to control the sexual relationship and to determine how far sexual activity should go.

Peplau et al. also found differences between couples having sex early in a relationship and those waiting longer to have sex. Early sex couples were more likely to have had prior coital experience in a previous relationship. They were more accepting of sex without affection and gave more importance to sex as a dating goal.

One common myth about the sexual behaviour of young people is that they engage in sexual behaviour on a frequent basis. In fact, the opposite is true. For most of our sample intercourse was an infrequent experience with one-third of the sexually experienced females having intercourse once a month or less. Sexual relations were even less frequent for the sexually experienced males of whom 70% of high school males and 58% of the college males had intercourse once a month or less. Only ten percent of the females and nine percent of the males had sexual relations three or more times a week.

Among high school students in Calgary about 60% of the sexually experienced had intercourse less than once a month (Meikle et al., 1981). Only 12% of the girls and 6% of the boys were having intercourse more than once a week. The frequency increased with age as 11% of 18 year olds were having sex more than once a week compared with only 2.5% of 14 year olds.

A distinction needs to be made between being sexually experienced and being sexually active. Many of the young people who have experienced sexual intercourse are not currently in a sexual relationship. Among high school students in London, Ontario one-half of the sexually experienced had not experienced intercourse during the previous six weeks (Stennett et al., 1975).

Where do young people usually have sex? A study of pregnant teenage girls by Dr. Cowell (1975) in Toronto found that for 60% of the girls intercourse most often occurred in the boyfriend's home. For 15% it was most often at the girl's home and for 9% it occurred at a friend's house. Only 3% said they had intercourse in a car. In Saskatchewan, Weston (1980) found that for first intercourse the most likely places were in one's own home, in one's partner's home or in a car.

In the Toronto study sexual encounters often occurred in the home while the parents were absent, especially during the daytime when both parents were away at work. Its common occurrence in the boyfriend's house has considerable implications for contraceptive use and suggests the necessity of emphasizing male contraceptive responsibility in sex education programs. Females are more reluctant to have intercourse in their own home than in their boyfriend's home because they are more concerned about their own parents possibly finding out than they are about being discovered by the boyfriend's parents. Also, many females, especially those who are close to their parents, might feel too guilty to have sex in the parental home. Being at home might remind them of their parents' negative views regarding premarital sex.

Perception of the Sexual Experience of Others

What perception do young people have of the sexual experience of others? The students in our research were asked to indicate the percentage of high school students they thought would experience premarital intercourse before leaving high school and to give separate estimates for males and females. Both sexes estimated that a greater proportion of males than females would experience premarital intercourse. This reflects the common stereotype in our society that males are more sexually experienced than are females. The nonvirgins gave considerably higher estimates of sexual activity than did the virgins. Among the males, 70% of the nonvirgins estimated that more than 40% of males would experience intercourse before leaving high school whereas only one-third of the virgins gave this high an estimate. Among females, about twice as many nonvirgins (58%) as virgins (33%) estimated that more than 40% of females would experience intercourse before leaving high school.

Teenagers often have an inaccurate idea as to the extent of premarital sexual activity among their age group. One reason for this is that young people tend to associate with others having similar ideas and values so that those who experience premarital sex are likely to associate with others experiencing premarital sex and consequently will believe that almost everyone is having premarital sex. On the other hand, adamant virgins who are strongly opposed to premarital sex are unlikely to be friends with those who hold a contrary view. Also people are likely to share their sexual experience with others only if they believe the others will be supportive. It is unlikely that a sexually experienced woman would tell an adamant virgin about her sexual activity because she knows that the other person would disapprove.

With regard to opposite sex estimates, both virgin and nonvirgin males estimated fewer women as having experienced premarital sex than the females themselves did. For example, while 33% of the virgin females estimated that more than 40% of females would experience intercourse before leaving high school, only 18% of the virgin males gave this estimate. There was even a greater discrepancy in estimates of male sexual experience. Whereas two-thirds of the female virgins estimated that more than 40% of the males would experience intercourse before leaving high school, only one-third of the virgin males gave this estimate. Women may overestimate male sexual experience because they believe it is easier for males to become sexually involved. Males underestimate female sexual activity possibly because based on their own experience they have had more women reject than accept their sexual advances.

Reasons for Having Intercourse

Given the widespread acceptance of premarital intercourse in a love relationship, many young people view sexual intercourse as a natural extension of their dating relationship. However, males are more likely to emphasize sexual rather than relationship reasons for having sex. Hobart (1975) in asking university students to justify their first sexual experience found that males were twice as likely as females to give as a reason the strength of their sexual drive than saying it was an expression of love for their partner. For women the most important reason was that sex was a natural expression of their love for their partner while strength of sex drive was second in importance. Several also mentioned curiosity. A typical comment from a university female in our study was:

> *Sexual intercourse was for me mainly an expression of the love I felt for my partner whom I wanted to satisfy. Also in a more minor way it satisfied an intense curiosity I had about sexual intercourse.*

The availability of birth control is seldom, if ever, mentioned as a reason for engaging in premarital sex. In one study where young people were asked about the influence of birth control (Cvetkovich and Grote, 1977), it was rated as the least important reason by both sexes. This suggests that providing contraceptive devices does not encourage premarital sexual activity.

With the greater acceptability of premarital sex today, some young people view virginity as an undesirable burden. This attitude seems more common among those whose friends have all experienced intercourse. One 19-year-old female stated:

> *I couldn't stand the fact that I was the only virgin remaining among my circle of friends and so I decided to have sex with the first male who looked promising even though I hardly knew him.*

Although older adolescents are likely to engage in premarital sex because of mutual desire, this is not as true for younger females who are more likely to do it because of pressure from their boyfriend. In a study of young pregnant adolescents, Steinhoff (1976) found that most young girls did not enjoy sexual relations but said they were worried the boyfriend might break off the dating relationship if they didn't go along with him. Similarly Miller and Simon (1974) found among young girls that the concern was not sexual gratification but to maintain the dating relationship. One 15-year-old girl in our study said:

> *If you're going with a guy and you don't have sex and he wants it you'll probably break up. You know you won't last very long.*

Reactions to First Intercourse

Societal attitudes greatly influence the reactions of young people to their first sexual experience. Where premarital sex is favourably looked upon, young people are generally positive about their first sexual experience. On the other hand, if premarital sex is condemned, sexually active adolescents usually develop strong guilt feelings. Christensen (1969) has proposed a theory of relative consequences which states that the effects of premarital sexual behaviour are dependent upon cultural norms and that the negative consequences are greatest in restrictive societies. This theory accounts for the fact that guilt over premarital sex is greatest in societies which disapprove of premarital sex. This is also true for subgroups within society. For example, Perlman (1978) found sexually experienced students from a religious college to be more guilty than students from the University of Manitoba where premarital sex was more accepted.

Despite increasing acceptance of premarital sex, many young Canadians still report guilt feelings when they first experience premarital intercourse. Fifty-six percent of the women and 33% of the men in our student study had guilt feelings at first intercourse. This guilt resulted from the violation of the standards of significant others such as parents or peers as well as from the violation of their own personal standards. A typical response was that of a high school female who stated:

> When I first had premarital sex I experienced tremendous guilt. I worried about being caught and what my parents' reaction would be if they ever found out. I was bothered by the fact that I would never again be a virgin. Because of these feelings, I had a low opinion of myself.

A university female commented:

> After having intercourse for the first time I felt that what I had done was wrong for it went against my religion and my parents' views, but at the same time felt the need to secure my boyfriend's love.

Hobart (1975) found among Alberta students that several women who felt guilty about first intercourse were pressured into having coitus by their partner. Most of these women were from poor economic backgrounds and closely tied to their parents. They were also religiously devout. The most common reasons they gave for feeling guilty were violation of morals, loss of virginity they would have preferred to save for their spouse, break-up of the relationship with their first sexual partner and not being in love with their sexual partner. Males most often gave the reasons of violation of morals, fear of pregnancy and not loving their partner.

Once young people begin having premarital sex, few discontinue that behaviour because of guilt feelings. Instead, with increasing sexual experience, guilt tends to diminish. This is particularly true for those who are in love relationship and who believe that love makes sex moral.

During my third year at university I had my first experiences with premarital intercourse. My partner was someone I had been dating for about six months previously, and there was a strong love relationship involved. In many ways I think this bond of affection helped to make it a positive experience.

In our student study only 18% of the females and 10% of the males said they currently felt guilty. For females highest guilt was among those:

who disapproved of premarital intercourse
whose parents disapproved of premarital intercourse
whose friends disapproved of premarital intercourse
who had premarital intercourse less often.

Of the variables related to guilt, the one of friends' attitudes had the strongest relationship. For example, of those whose friends disapproved of premarital sex, 47% currently felt guilty whereas among those whose friends were approving of premarital sex only 10% felt guilty.

None of these four factors were significantly related to guilt among males. Probably one of the key reasons for this is that so few males felt guilty. Also almost all of the males as well as their friends approved of premarital sex. In addition, males are less likely than females to be concerned about parental reactions to their engaging in premarital sex.

An important reason for understanding the nature of sexual guilt is that guilty adolescents are not likely to use effective birth control when engaging in intercourse. This will be discussed more fully in the chapter on contraceptive use and non-use.

Another common reaction to first intercourse, particularly among females, is that of disappointment either because it was not as pleasurable as they thought it would be or because it was painful. In a survey of 37 university females I found that one-half said their first intercourse experience was painful. Also, few women achieved an orgasm the first time they had intercourse. The following is a typical comment:

My first intercourse was a great disappointment because I did not achieve an orgasm. I had found masturbation to be highly pleasurable and assumed that intercourse would be even more pleasurable.

Another stated:

What compelled me to have intercourse was the desire to experience the ultimate orgasm in intercourse. I had read many sensational descriptions of orgasm which was a beautiful experience for the couple. However, this first intercourse did not meet my expectations. Afterwards, I had mixed feelings of disappointment as well as being glad that I had lost my virginity.

Hass (1979) found there were significant differences in the concerns that males and females had over first intercourse. The boys were most concerned with performing well and being a good lover. The girls were concerned primarily with pain, the possibility of pregnancy and fear of acquiring a loose reputation.

The characteristics of the partner strongly influence the female's reaction to first intercourse. Weiss (1973) found that university females felt more positive about their first intercourse experience if their partner was loving and considerate. This was more important than whether or not that partner was one they had just met or one they were engaged to marry.

Despite the considerable amount of nervousness, anxiety and guilt surrounding first intercourse, most young people react to the loss of virginity as a positive step in the development of their personal maturity. In Hobart's (1975) study 75% of the university students said their first experience was a "good one." Although the initial experience may not have met their expectations, a common reaction reported by young males and females is the feeling of changing their identity and becoming more of an adult. Some express a sense of relief at finally having "done it". Whitehurst (1972), in interviewing female students at the University of Windsor, found that most of them felt they had become "more of a woman" as a result of the experience. Similar reactions have been given by women in our research:

Intercourse was a natural development of our relationship as far as I was concerned. The experience made me feel that now I was a woman, whereas before I had only been a girl.

I thought that being a virgin symbolized being an old maid or a sexually undesirable woman. Because of this I was glad to lose my virginity.

Upon returning home that evening I examined myself closely in the mirror to see if there were any noticeable differences in my appearance. Since I was no longer a virgin I wondered whether others would notice that I had reached a new stage in my development. I felt I had expanded my sexual identity and would see myself in a new way. I thought, aren't I supposed to feel guilt, remorse, shame? But I don't. I feel perfectly normal and I don't regret it. It isn't dirty or bad. I feel like a whole person capable of making my own decisions about what I do.

Reasons for Not Having Premarital Intercourse

Until recently most young people have been deterred from premarital sex because of moral objections. However, in our student study the two most important reasons given by virgins for sexual abstention were that either they did not feel ready to have premarital intercourse or else they had not met the right person. One-half of the students gave one or the other of these reasons. One-third of both sexes listed moral reasons such as religious beliefs or the belief that intercourse before marriage is wrong. Next in importance for males (16%) was that the partner was not willing to engage in premarital sex. Only 1% of females said the partner was not willing. More females (10%) than males (4%) gave fear of pregnancy and only 3% of females and none of the males said fear of parental disapproval was the most important reason.

Thus young people who do not engage in premarital sex make this decision more often because of personal growth or opportunity reasons than because of moral constraints. The key reasons are that they are not ready to have intercourse or that they have not met the right person.

Those who gave moral reasons for sexual abstention were more devoutly religious than those who have other reasons. Among the virgin females who attended church once a week or more, two-thirds gave moral reasons for abstaining as compared with 5% who said they never attended church. For males, one-half of those who attended church once a week or more gave moral reasons compared with 20% of those who never attended. Involvement in a dating relationship also significantly influenced the type of reasons given. Most males who were in a committed relationship had experienced intercourse. Among the few virgin males who were in a committed dating relationship 88% gave moral reasons for abstaining compared with only 19% of those who were currently not dating. Among virgin women in a committed relationship there were as many who said they were not ready as there were who gave moral reasons for abstaining. Virgin women who were not dating were divided between reasons of morality and not having met the right person.

There was a strong relationship between the type of reasons given for not engaging in premarital intercourse and the probability of engaging in coitus in the future. All of the males and 99% of the females who gave moral reasons said they were not likely to have premarital sex. In contrast, of those who said they had not yet met the right person, 76% of males and 59% of the females indicated that they were likely to have premarital intercourse.

Although fear of pregnancy was not given as a major reason for refraining from ever having intercourse, most young people do worry about the possibility of becoming pregnant. In Saskatchewan, Weston (1980), found that one-half of the sexually experienced teenagers had at some time refrained from having intercourse because of fear of pregnancy.

Loss of reputation was not given as one of the major factors deterring premarital sex. Most young people believe that if they are in love then having sexual relations would be acceptable to their peers. However, loss of reputation is a key factor deterring young women from engaging in casual sexual relations with many partners. A concern of many women is the possibility of their sexual partners talking about them and ridiculing them. Some comments from high school females were:

Who wants to be classified as "easy" by the rest of the school?

A lot of girls can't enjoy sex because they're afraid that the guy will blab about everything . . . and of course it would all be exaggerated!

It's not fair. You always have to watch how much you give a guy. You always have to keep in mind what'll be said about you in the locker room.

Many young women worry that if they acquire a label as being promiscuous or "loose" then males will only be interested in them for sex and they will have a difficult time establishing a serious dating relationship with someone they like. Hass (1979) found that most teenage males did not approve of females who had had many sexual partners. In addition to having a low evaluation of such females, boys worry that a girl with considerable previous experience might compare them with her other sexual partners.

Non-Coital
Sexual Behaviour

Society puts a great deal of emphasis on virginity, so that sexuality is often equated with intercourse. Thus, it is sometimes assumed that young people who have not experienced intercourse are not engaging in any sexual behaviour. In fact, most young people, even those who have not experienced intercourse, do engage in some sexual activity.

Petting

Hobart (1972) in his study of university students in three Canadian provinces found that more than 90% had petted and 80% had experienced petting below the waist. Similarly, at the University of Manitoba, Perlman (1978) found that about 90% of the male and female students accepted petting in a love relationship. In Saskatchewan, Weston (1980) found that three-quarters of 15 to 19 year olds had engaged in light petting i.e. breast stimulation with the average age of beginning this activity being 14 years, 8 months. Sixty-three percent had experienced heavy petting, defined for the female as letting a guy play with her vagina and for the male as playing with a girl's vagina. The average age at which heavy petting first occurred was 15 years.

Although there is general acceptance of petting among young people, there is also considerable anxiety about it, especially among younger adolescents. Young people may be confused about what is actually involved in petting and whether or not their petting behaviour is acceptable. These university females commented:

Although I passively engaged in some petting, I felt absolutely no sexual arousal, and only did it to please the guys. I never felt upset because I didn't experience any arousal. I didn't know I was supposed to.

As our petting experiences became heavier I managed to have my first orgasm with a man—and I cried. The orgasm itself felt great, but my guilt took over and turned it into a sickening experience.

Before experiencing petting I never actually knew what it was. Once I started petting I enjoyed it yet I felt a great deal of anxiety and guilt about it. I particularly wondered if it was normal to pet. Fortunately one day I was able to discuss this with my cousin and she assured me that petting was normal and healthy. This was a tremendous relief because I thought I had been doing something bad or unhealthy. I was relieved to find out other girls had sexual urges and enjoyed petting.

Most couples proceed from lighter to more intimate types of petting in a fairly standard sequence. The usual stages are kissing, fondling of the breasts and manual stimulation of the genitals. For some couples oral sex precedes intercourse while for others it does not occur until after intercourse has been experienced.

The greatest change in petting behaviour among young people has been the widespread acceptance of oral sex. If we refer to the acceptance of premarital intercourse as the first sexual revolution, then the second sexual revolution would certainly be the acceptance of oral sex. During the 1970's there was more open discussion of this topic than during previous decades. Shere Hite (1976) in her research on female sexuality found that a high proportion of women achieved greater sexual gratification from oral sex than intercourse. She also found that many women could more easily obtain an orgasm through oral sex than through intercourse.

In his study of adolescents, Hass (1979) found that almost all of the boys who had experienced fellatio said it was very pleasurable. However, females were more likely to feel uneasy about cunnilingus. Although for some females it was a totally pleasurable experience, for others who were ambivalent it was mainly because of negative feelings about their genitals. Thus girls tended to worry more about whether or not the partner was really enjoying it. In the same study girls also reported greater enjoyment when a boy manually stimulated their genitals than when they touched a boy's penis. Boys, on the other hand, reported equal enjoyment for these two activities.

In one study, we asked 200 university females questions about oral sex (Herold & Way, 1983). Sixty-one percent had performed oral sex on a male and 68% said a male had performed oral sex on them. The fact that women are just as likely to give as to receive oral sex is a reflection of the changing expectancies surrounding female sexual behaviour. Whereas previously women took a generally passive role in sexual relations, women today expect to play the role of an active participant in activities such as oral sex.

Oral sex occurred relatively infrequently with only 39% of the experienced women indicating they had engaged in oral sex once a week or more during the previous month. Twenty-six percent had not engaged in oral sex during the previous month. Of those who had experienced intercourse, 97% had engaged in oral sex. Among those who had not experienced intercourse, one-third had engaged in oral sex. Within this virgin group more women had received oral sex (35%) than had given oral sex (26%). One-half of the women had brought their partners to orgasm through oral sex and one-half had themselves reached orgasm from their partner's oral stimulation.

The fact that one-third of virgins had experienced oral sex indicates that many consider oral sex as less intimate than complete intercourse. This is a significant change from the 1940's and 1950's when Kinsey reported that oral sex was unlikely to take place unless intercourse had first occurred.

Only 19% of those who had experienced oral sex felt guilty about it. However, of those who had not experienced oral sex 81% said they would feel guilty if they did engage in it.

Few of the subjects had any type of discussion regarding oral sex with their parents. Only 16% had discussed the topic with their mothers and 3% had discussed this with their fathers. Even when discussions were held with parents the topic was discussed only in general terms. Sixty-one percent had discussed oral sex with a close friend and 70% had discussed the topic with their dating partner. The level of disclosure was far greater to the dating partner than to the close friend as 38% indicated disclosing in complete detail to their dating partner but only 13% said they disclosed in complete detail to their close friend. Self-disclosure to the dating partner regarding oral sex experience was significantly related to experience with oral sex as those who had experienced oral sex were more willing to talk to the partner about oral sex than were those who had never experienced oral sex.

For young people whose values prohibit premarital intercourse or who are not ready for premarital intercourse, petting is a means of accommodating both the prohibition against sexual intercourse and the desire for sexual relations. University females commented:

Sex to me was synonymous with intercourse and petting of any kind was a means of distracting and consoling my partner so he would not dwell on his frustration over my refusals.

Although I am a strong Catholic and cannot accept premarital intercourse, I do enjoy petting to orgasm and believe it is a satisfactory substitute for intercourse.

One 18-year-old high school student who had been raised in a conservative fundamentalist environment stated she could not accept premarital intercourse because of the strong stand her church had taken on this issue. Nevertheless, she engaged in considerable sexual activity with her boyfriend including manual and oral stimulation to orgasm. She rationalized that while her church prohibited vaginal intercourse, it had not specifically forbidden other types of sexual activities. This young woman represents what is known as a "technical virgin".

Although there is a debate over the value of technical virginity, more experts are promoting petting to orgasm as a satisfactory substitute for sexual intercourse. Eleanor Hamilton (1978) argues that by petting to orgasm young people can relieve their sexual frustrations and can better understand each other's sexual response pattern. Some young people who fear pregnancy and are not prepared to use contraception are substituting intimate petting for intercourse:

After a pregnancy scare I refused to have intercourse for about six months but would allow petting and oral-genital stimulation.

Masturbation

Masturbation or the sexual self-stimulation of the genitals is a common sexual practice among young people. In one study of university students researchers found that almost all males and two-thirds of females had engaged in masturbation (Arafat and Cotton, 1974). A difference between male and female masturbation is that most males begin masturbating in early adolescence whereas most females do not begin until middle or later adolescence. Another difference is that whereas almost all males who masturbate do so to orgasm, about one-third of females who masturbate do not have an orgasm. A possible explanation is that many young women feel uncomfortable about sexually stimulating their gentials and therefore are less able to stimulate themselves to orgasm.

I never considered that masturbation was for me. Actually, I thought that only prostitutes, oversexed, or sexually deprived people did it. I made attempts at touching my clitoris, but it either became so sensitive or I sensed guilt for even trying to manipulate my genitals for such a reason.

Although there is a general awareness that masturbation is a common practice among young males, many people do not believe females have a need to masturbate. Parents are generally more concerned about and more discouraging of their daughter's masturbation than their son's masturbation. Consequently, females who engage in masturbation may think of themselves as abnormal or different and believe that they are "the only ones doing it." Although many women experience masturbation, this topic is not usually discussed with others. In a study of sexual self-disclosure we found that masturbation was the least likely of any sexual activity to be discussed with others. Female comments were:

Masturbation is about the only taboo subject still remaining among my women friends at university. Sexual arousal may be discussed perhaps, but only at a non-personal level and usually as part of a joke. Masturbation does not even reach this level of acceptance in conversation.

When I first began masturbating I thought it was a perverted practice and found it hard to believe that other women might masturbate.

Our research indicates that about two-thirds of university females have ever masturbated. There is a strong relationship between age and having experienced masturbation as 80% of 22-year-old females said they had experienced masturbation compared to 40% of 19-year-olds.

Although masturbation is commonly practiced among males, most males, if given the choice, say they would prefer intercourse to masturbation. However, some females would rather engage in masturbation than have sex in a relationship where they were not comfortable.

When I first started petting I would not permit my boyfriend to bring me to orgasm because this would make me feel too guilty. Instead I masturbated to orgasm after our dates.

When I was a teenager I could not morally accept having intercourse with a male to whom I was attracted but had no particular relationship with. So I would engage in masturbation instead.

Although there is a greater acceptance of masturbation today than in previous years, there is still considerable discomfort with it. In our research 25% of the women who had ever masturbated said they felt guilty about it. Of those who had never masturbated 70% said they would feel guilty if they did. Younger teenagers in particular are more likely to have greater anxieties about masturbation.

Some female comments were:

I worried that masturbation would affect my ability to have intercourse or to bear children. I felt I was abnormal to have such a strong sex drive as to want release through masturbation.

My main worry about masturbation was that I might damage myself or become pregnant. At one time I thought that my menstrual cramps were a result of my masturbation.

I was deeply concerned that I was deformed, perhaps from masturbating, because one side of my labia was grossly larger than the other.

Masturbation had been a major source of guilt throughout my sexual development and I blamed many of my problems such as delayed physical development and lack of enjoyment of my initial heterosexual experiences as punishment from God for being "perverted".

A male commented:

My main concern about masturbation was fear I would get caught. Also I wondered if I was harming myself, for example, I thought my wet dreams were a result of my masturbation.

Another concern is over the frequency of masturbation. Often teenagers worry that they masturbate more than their peers and perceive there is something abnormal about their sex drive. In fact, there is a considerable variation in frequency of masturbation. Among those who masturbate, some do it on a daily basis and others do it only once or twice a year. Among university females who had masturbated, we found that one-third had not masturbated in the previous month and 22% were masturbating once a week or more.

Although masturbation is usually practiced to relieve sexual frustration, adolescents also can use masturbation for other purposes.

Some women find masturbation helpful in alleviating menstrual cramps. Some students use it to relieve tension such as around examination time. One male stated:

I find that when I am tense masturbation can help me to relax or help me to fall asleep.

Many adolescent males and females learn about masturbation through self-discovery. Males often find out from their friends. Some females learn about masturbation after having the experience of being petted to orgasm by a dating partner. Others learn about the subject from books or magazines.

Probably the greatest change regarding masturbation has been the acceptance and encouragement of female masturbation. Feminists and many health professionals during the 1970's were encouraging young women to masturbate to orgasm as a means of understanding their own sexuality and also as a means of asserting their own sexual freedom. Some women report that they receive more intense orgasm from masturbation than from intercourse. In sex therapy masturbation is often used as a means of assisting non-orgasmic women to achieve orgasm during their sexual relations.

Males differ in their acceptance of female masturbation. While some males find the idea of female masturbation highly stimulating, others believe there is something wrong with a woman who masturbates. Males with negative views may interpret masturbation as a reflection of inadequacy in either their own or their partner's lovemaking abilities.

Sexual Fantasies

Until a few years ago many psychiatrists believed that sexual fantasies were a sign of emotional disturbance or conflict. Today this is no longer seen as true for the great majority of people.

Most young people have thoughts or fantasies about engaging in sexual activity. In a study of American teenagers, Hass (1979) found that about 80% often thought or fantasized about sex. Boys differed from girls in the content of their fantasies with the boys having explicit fantasies about different sexual acts whereas the girls' fantasies were more romantic. Hass also found that sexually inexperienced teenagers had the most romantic fantasies with an emphasis on affection rather than sexual contact.

In a questionnaire survey of 137 single university women we found a high proportion of romantic rather than explicitly sexual fantasies (Pelletier & Herold, 1983). There was usually an emphasis on a romantic setting such as on a deserted beach or by the fire in a log cabin during a snow storm.

I like to think about being with my boyfriend and engaging in an all night bout of sex on a large bear skin rug, in front of a roaring fire in a cozy log cabin.

My favourite sexual fantasy is to be walking in the woods with a friend and feeling warm in the sunshine, lying in the leaves and then making love, after slowly undressing each other.

I'm probably the only 22 year old who still fantasizes about their wedding night. I like to think about getting ready for my first sexual experience. The sexual act is intense and exciting but the foreplay and the aftermath are most satisfying. Just being close and waking in his arms the morning after gives me a sense of fulfillment and perhaps security.

Almost all of the women had fantasized, with the most common fantasy (90%) being about having sexual intercourse with a boyfriend or future husband. Two-thirds had fantasies about oral sex. Many (78%) fantasized about previous sexual experiences.

Fifty-one percent had fantasies about being forced to engage in sex by a man. This fantasy reflects traditional sex role stereotypes whereby the male is the powerful aggressor and initiator of sex and the woman is the passive recipient of his advances. Although this forced sex fantasy appeals to many women as a fantasy, in real life, women do not want this to happen to them.

I have fantasized once being raped by a male that I don't know. This male is very gentle with me and doesn't hurt me. He ties my hands and feet to the bedposts and then very slowly kisses me all over my body, gradually leading up to oral sex.

A minority of the women fantasized about their being in control of the situation.

One fantasy I have is that I will be able to 'seduce' the man of my choice— whether he be someone I know or a complete stranger. I would like to be totally in control of the situation and call all the shots. In my fantasy, the man would not be able to resist me.

When asked about the situations in which they fantasized, 84% said they fantasized in non-sexual situations. Of those who had experienced intercourse, 28% never fantasized during intercourse, 32% seldom fantasized and 40% sometimes or usually fantasized during intercourse. Fantasizing during masturbation was very common. Of those who had ever masturbated, only 19% seldom or never fantasized during masturbation, 24% sometimes fantasized and 57% usually or always fantasized during masturbation.

I would not enjoy masturbation (or even intercourse) as much if I did not fantasize. I always fantasize when masturbating and during sexual intercourse with my boyfriend. Most of my fantasies centre on intercourse and oral sex with males.

Sexual fantasies can serve to heighten sexual functioning as 48% had fantasized to become sexually aroused and 30% fantasized to help achieve orgasm. Fantasizing can also be useful in non-sexual situations. For example, about one-half of the women had used sexual fantasies as a means of helping them to fall asleep. Finally, 73% said they fantasized because it was "a pleasant pastime".

Most felt comfortable about having sexual fantasies as only 10% said they had guilt feelings about them. However, for a few, sexual fantasies caused considerable guilt or were inhibited by guilt.

I attended weekly church services in a state of panic that I may possibly have committed a sin by having sexual thoughts or merely by allowing my sexual thoughts to emerge as a questioning of my faith.

I cannot recall ever having any sexual fantasies as a teen. I feel that perhaps I did not have any as a direct result of my unhappy petting experiences. I was guilt-ridden and anxious, and this no doubt inhibited my sexual fantasies from occurring.

There were significant differences between the fantasies of sexually experienced and inexperienced women. Women with more sexual experience and who had less sexual guilt had a greater number of different types of fantasies, fantasized more often and had more explicitly erotic fantasies. These results suggest that sexual experience serves to increase one's fantasy life rather than to diminish it.

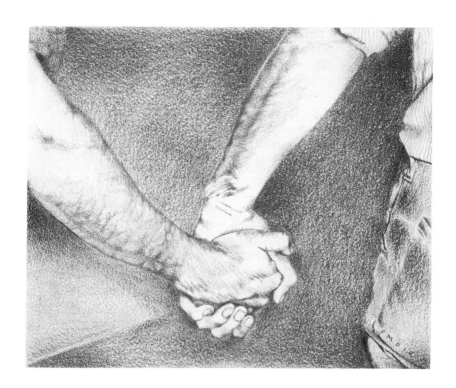

Homosexuality

The word homosexual can be used to mean either sexual behaviour between persons of the same sex or a sexual preference for the same sex. This distinction is important because one might be attracted to and even have a sexual preference for someone of the same sex without engaging in homosexual behaviour. Also, a person may engage in homosexual behaviour and yet have a sexual preference for the opposite sex. Furthermore, preferences in behaviours may change over time so that an individual might have a heterosexual preference at one time and a homosexual preference at another time. Kinsey and his associates (1948) thus proposed that heterosexuality and homosexuality were not exclusive entities but should be ranked on a continuum at the mid-point of which would be bisexuals who are equally attracted to people of either sex.

Homosexuality can also be used as an identity label by which a person defines himself as a homosexual. Many homosexuals prefer to use the term "gay" to describe this identity. Some people may engage in homosexual behaviour and yet define themselves as heterosexual. Others may define themselves as homosexual but keep this identity hidden from others because of fear of censure if this identity were to be made public. In another category are those who accept their homosexual identity and openly reveal this to others. For this latter group homosexuality is generally not only a form of behaviour but a lifestyle in which almost all of one's social and recreational activities are spent within the gay community. The term "homophile" is used to refer to the totality of this homosexual life style.

Young people are confused about homosexuality and may believe that if they have engaged in any homosexual experience, this means they are homosexual. In fact, prior to and around the time of puberty many young people engage in homosexual experimentation out of curiosity and because they are denied the outlet of heterosexual expression. It usually occurs only a few times with one or two partners (Hunt, 1974). This is more likely to occur in single-sex institutions such as private schools.

Young people who engage in this homosexual experimentation may not think of themselves as homosexual, however, they may be concerned about others labelling them as such if their activity were to be later discovered. When they become older many adolescents feel embarrassed and guilty about their earlier homosexual experiences.

While recurring homosexual fantasies may indicate a definite same sex preference this is not necessarily true. It is not uncommon for young people to have some sexual thoughts or fantasies about someone of the same sex. In a study of university females we found that 18% had experienced homosexual fantasies (Herold & Pelletier, 1983). Young people can be troubled by such fantasies and wonder if this is a sign that they are homosexual. One university female stated:

> *I sometimes used to fantasize about a woman who was naked above the waist and I would fondle her breasts. I found this fantasy very arousing but worried that it might mean I was a homosexual. In real life I find the idea of having sex with another woman to be repulsive and I cannot image myself ever doing it.*

In our society women have been presented as being more sexually attractive than males. Not surprisingly, some women are sexually aroused by other women's bodies. Comments from two university females were:

> *I have always found pictures of nude females to be more of a turn-on than pictures of nude males. A couple of times I have looked at the male pictures in Playgirl magazine but have had no reaction to them. While I have only occasionally looked at Playboy magazine the pictures there are a lot more interesting to me than those in Playgirl. This used to make me wonder if I were a lesbian.*

> *That I was aroused by pictures of nude women in magazines heightened my fears of being abnormal and practically had me convinced that I was a lesbian. Oppressed with thoughts of being a homosexual, I prayed that God would help me to change and become more normal.*

Anxieties about one's homosexual identity can also occur if young people are sexually propositioned by someone of the same sex. They might believe that they may have unconsciously given some signal indicating their interest. One time after a university class at which a group of homosexuals had spoken, one student commented that she avoided looking directly at the group for fear they might think she was gay.

It is difficult to know accurately the proportion of people who are exclusively homosexual. Kinsey reported that about four percent of American males and one to two percent of American females were exclusively homosexual with considerably higher percentages having had some homosexual experience (Kinsey et al., 1948; Kinsey et al., 1953). In Toronto Barrett (1980b) found that 16.5% of university males and seven percent of university females reported some post-pubertal homosexual contact. In my research with university females eight percent reported some homosexual contact after puberty. Generally these were rare occurrences and very few were exclusively homosexual.

Among most homosexuals the adolescent period is the most trying one in their lives as there are strong peer pressures to be seen as normal in the sense of being heterosexual and going out on dates with someone of the opposite sex. In fact, many homosexuals do date members of the opposite sex.

Adolescents can be cruel to others who appear different and this is especially true when others appear to be different sexually. Some of the most derogatory terms used by young people are those referring to homosexuals such as "queer", or "fag". Fear of peer rejection leads to feelings of tremendous isolation and often the homosexually oriented adolescent feels he has no one to turn to to discuss his sexual concerns.

When a person comes to accept his or her identity as a homosexual, this is referred to as "coming out". The process of "coming out" generally occurs earlier for homosexual males than for females. This stage is most likely to occur when the individual becomes involved in the homosexual community or falls in love with someone who is homosexual (Dank, 1971). For many this coming out process can take several years and a sizeable proportion of men and women wait until after they have been married and have had children before coming to accept their homosexual identity (Bell & Weinberg, 1978). While "coming out" may be terrifying it can also provide emotional relief in the sense that the person has finally resolved his/her sexual identity (Dank, 1971).

Our society has commonly accepted stereotypes of what homosexual males or lesbian women are like. Yet there is as great a diversity among homosexuals as there is among heterosexuals. Bell and Weinberg (1978), in one of the largest studies of homosexuals in the United States, found that most fell into five distinct life-style categories: (1) The close-coupled homosexuals lived a monogamous life-style with one partner. The relationship resembled that of a married heterosexual couple. They had the fewest sexual problems and were the most satisfied with their sexual lives. (2) The open-coupled homosexuals had one special sexual partner but they were likely to seek other sexual partners. (3) Functional homosexuals preferred to live by themselves and they engaged in frequent sexual activity with many partners. (4) Dysfunctional homosexuals were not in a couple relationship. They regretted their homosexuality, reported more sexual problems than the other groups and considered themselves as sexually unappealing. (5) Asexual homosexuals were the most socially isolated. They had few partners, engaged in little sexual activity and most of their leisure time was spent alone.

There are considerable differences between the sexual experiences of male and female homosexuals, particularly with respect to the number of sexual partners. In the American study by Bell and Weinberg (1978), seventy-four percent of the males but only two percent of the females had experienced sexual relations with one hundred or more homosexual partners. Most of the male sexual contacts were with complete strangers whereas hardly any of the female contacts were with strangers. Bell and Weinberg (1978), also found that lesbian relationships tended to last longer than the relationships of male homosexuals.

Lesbians tend to focus more on the emotional aspects of their relationships than on the sexual aspects. During the adolescent years lesbian females are similar to heterosexual females in that their sexual fantasies focus more on love and romance than on sexual behaviour. Initial homosexual interaction among adolescent girls is more likely to involve affectionate kissing and caressing than it is among young adolescent boys (Saghir & Robins, 1983).

One impact of the sexual life-style of homosexual males can be seen in the incidence of sexually transmitted diseases (STDs). Bell and Weinberg (1978) found that two-thirds of homosexual males but none of the homosexual females had ever contracted an STD from a person of the same sex. Homosexual males also have a much higher rate of STDs than do heterosexual males. There are a number of diseases which appear to be sexually transmitted primarily by homosexual males, but which have not been labeled as STDs. Some of these diseases, such as hepatitis B and intestinal parasites, are a consequence of anal sexual activity. In Toronto a controlled study of 200 homosexual men and 100 heterosexual men found that two-thirds of the homosexual men but only sixteen percent of the heterosexual men were infected with intestinal parasites (Keystone, Keystone & Proctore, 1980).

The STD which is by far the most dangerous and which has received the most publicity is AIDS (Acquired Immune Deficiency). The AIDS epidemic, because it is life-threatening, has thrown panic into the gay community and is causing some to re-assess their attitudes to casual sex.

The key factor accounting for the high rate of STDs among homosexual males is the numerous casual and anonymous sexual contacts within the homosexual community. STD control is extremely difficult because anonymous sex makes it impossible to trace sexual partners who may be spreading the diseases.

There are three basic views regarding homosexuality. One view is that homosexuality is sinful and that to maintain the moral fabric of society those who engage in homosexual acts should be punished. Those who accept this view tend to believe that restrictions in employment and other areas need to be placed on homosexuals to prevent them from recruiting others, especially among young people, into the gay life style.

Another view is that homosexuals are sick people who should seek treatment to be cured. Because case studies by psychiatrists portrayed homosexuals as having serious personality problems, homosexuality was defined as a form of mental illness. However, when researchers compared nonpatient homosexuals with heterosexuals, it was concluded that homosexuals did not have more personal problems than heterosexuals (Hooker, 1957). As of 1974 the American Psychiatric Association no longer considers homosexuality as an illness.

The third view is that homosexuality is an acceptable alternative form of behaviour and that human rights of homosexuals should be protected. According to this view the problems faced by homosexuals are primarily a consequence of negative attitudes held by the larger society toward homosexuality. Given these conflicting views it is not surprising that homosexuality has become an emotionally charged political and legal issue. Examples of this can be seen in the raids by Toronto police on gay bath houses and the obscenity charges placed by the Ontario Government against the gay magazine *The Body Politic*.

In general, our society has strong negative attitudes toward homosexuality and particularly male homosexuality. In one study of university students in Waterloo, those who held conservative views on a diversity of sexual issues were also more likely to hold negative views toward homosexuality (Dunbar, Brown & Amoroso, 1973). Those holding the strongest negative views also held stronger stereotypes of masculinity and femininity and were more willing to label a male homosexual if he exhibited what they believed was a feminine characteristic.

What are the origins of homosexuality? At one time researchers tried to find "the one major cause" of homosexuality. However, because researchers have been unable to prove the existence of a single cause there is increasing acceptance of the idea that homosexuality may have a diversity of origins.

Three major theories of homosexuality are the biological, the psychological, and the behavioural (Masters, Johnston and Kolodny, 1982). The biological approach encompasses both genetic and hormonal explanations. The genetic interpretation is that homosexuals are born with genes which predispose them to homosexuality. The hormonal explanation is that prior to birth, prenatal hormones can influence brain development predisposing a child to homosexuality. The psychological theory postulates that homosexuality results from faulty relationships with parents, for example, having an overprotective, dominant mother and a weak father. Behavioural theory postulates that an individual can become conditioned to being a homosexual by having positive erotic experiences with someone of the same sex while having either no opportunities for such experiences with the opposite sex or even negative experiences with the opposite sex. The research evidence for each of these theories is inconclusive.

For homosexuals who view their homosexuality as a problem there are two alternative types of treatment strategies: (1) Conversion therapy aimed at converting homosexuals to heterosexuality; (2) Adjustment therapy aimed at helping homosexuals adjust to their sexual lifestyle. While some conversion therapy has been successful it requires highly committed individuals who strongly desire such a change (Masters et al., 1982). Conversion therapy is most successful with those who have had some enjoyable sexual relations with the opposite sex. Among those who are exclusively homosexual, very few seek conversion therapy. Rather, if this group seeks therapy, they desire counselling which will help them adjust to their homosexual identity. Within the gay community itself, many organizations have developed to assist such individuals with this type of adjustment. Such organizations are commonly found in the larger urban centers and on university and community college campuses.

A critical decision for homosexuals is whether to reveal their orientation to their family and face possible rejection. Therapy for the adolescent and his/her family may become necessary when the adolescent makes the decision to be open about a gay life style. Most families find it very difficult to be understanding, let alone supportive of this decision. It is a shock to the family system which almost always will need assistance from outside in the form of a skillful family therapist.

Adolescents who are undecided about their sexual orientation should seek counselling with a therapist who is neutral about homosexuality. This would exclude radical homosexuals who would like to convert all of the undecided to homosexuality. Also excluded as counsellors should be heterosexuals who are anti-homosexual and who believe that all homosexuals should be converted to heterosexuals.

Sexual therapists or other therapists trained in the skills of sexual orientation assessment factors and who are able to impart the kinds of information the adolescent needs for self reflection would be most ideal.

Relationship and Sexual Problems

Dating

Adolescents are dating and becoming involved in steady dating relationships at younger ages than previously. Bell and Coughey (1980) in the United States reported that the age at which adolescents first went steady declined from 17 in 1958 to 15.9 in 1978. Teenagers who begin dating at early ages are more likely to begin steady dating at earlier ages and subsequently more likely to become sexually involved at younger ages (Meikle et al., 1981). Dr. Cowell (1975) in her study of pregnant teenagers in Toronto found that they began dating at an average age of 13.5 years, began going steady at 14.2 years and began having intercourse at 15.1 years. Among Saskatchewan youths, Weston (1980) found the average age of the first date to be 13.8 years. In the Calgary high school study, 58% of the young people reported they began dating by age 13 (Meikle et al., 1981).

One of the strongest predictors of sexual involvement is the type of dating relationship. During the 1950's when couples engaged in intercourse it usually did not occur until the engagement stage of the relationship. Today, with the acceptance of the permissiveness with affection norm, more young couples are likely to begin having intercourse at the going steady stage. In an American study Bell and Coughey (1980) reported that 67% of college females going steady in 1978 had experienced intercourse compared with 15% in 1958.

Not all young people are successful at dating and some do not date until after high school. In the student study we found that one-third of high school males and females were not currently dating and only 28% were in a steady relationship. Among university females only 15% were not dating and 44% were in a steady relationship or engaged. Among the university males about one-third were not dating and 39% were in a steady relationship or engaged. In terms of dating frequency, about one-half of the students were dating once a week or more often.

A university female commented:

In high school I didn't go out on dates and my parents told me I should be going out with boys. I then began to worry and strongly wished I could have a boyfriend so as to appear normal.

We need to recognize that young people generally consider the love and intimacy aspects of the relationship as being more important than the erotic aspects. For many young people sexual expression whether it be petting or intercourse is seen as a natural development of their emotional closeness and having an intimate relationship is considered an essential prerequisite for a satisfying sexual relationship.

As one 18-year-old high school female stated:

For me the feelings of love and closeness with my partner are more important than the actual physical enjoyment of sexual intercourse.

Unfortunately, because professionals are concerned primarily with the problematic aspects of sexual relationships, the other dimensions of male-female relationships are often overlooked and not seen as a concern. Although dating is important to most young people, many have a difficult time finding a satisfying relationship. Despite the stereotyped notion of many adults who perceive dating among youth to be generally happy and carefree, many young people report considerable anxiety and unhappiness about their dating relationships. Feelings of shyness, self-consciousness and being ill-at-ease are commonplace. Adults tend to oversimplify these problems. Yet for many young people dating success is central to their feelings of self-esteem and personal happiness.

Sexual Problems

Sexual concerns and problems are common among young people. In a survey of 15 to 19 year olds in Saskatchewan, Weston (1980) found that only 11% reported no concerns about sex. In terms of specific issues over which the young people worried most, sex was ranked third behind concerns about the future and their physical attractiveness.

Norms or rules of behaviour provide guidelines so that individuals know what is acceptable and unacceptable behaviour. The most trying situations are when norms do not exist or when the norms are not widely agreed upon because then people are uncertain as to what is expected of them. Today young people are torn between the two contradictory norms of sexual abstinence and sexual fulfillment. On the one hand, they are urged by parents and other traditional groups to abstain from sexual involvement and if they do become sexually involved guilt feelings often arise. On the other hand, they are exposed to peer group and dating norms which often emphasize sexual gratification. In the past a young woman's major concern was to preserve her virginity; today there is considerable peer and partner pressure not only to engage in sexual relations but to be successful as a proficient lover. Young men and women who believe that most of their friends are sexually experienced when they themselves are not might view their virginity as a source of embarrassment. Males particularly may worry that they are not living up to the image of the successful male. Some may begin to worry that they are homosexual. Thus, while some young people suffer guilt feelings over violating the sexual norms of parents, others worry that their sexual performance is not as great as it should be.

The emphasis on being able to satisfy one's sexual partner has been accompanied by a flood of sexual help books giving advice on how to improve one's sexual technique. Until recently this was a male responsibility, however, increasingly young women are concerned about the pleasure their partner receives. Because of the emphasis on sexual technique, young men and women often worry about the reaction of their sexual partner and fear displaying awkwardness or ignorance.

In a study of American teenagers three-quarters of the males and females said they worried about how good a sexual partner they were (Hass, 1979). The main concern was the degree of pleasure experienced by the partner. Many feared being compared with past sexual partners and acquiring a reputation for being an inadequate lover. Several worried their sexual inadequacy would result in their partner breaking off the relationship and choosing someone else. Some males preferred an inexperienced female so that there could be no comparison with previous lovers. Particularly in a casual sex situation the male was likely to feel that his partner had considerable sexual experience and that she might be judging his performance.

Among males two major sexual problems are premature ejaculation and impotency. Premature ejaculation refers to the male's involuntarily reaching orgasm very soon after insertion of his penis into the vagina. Premature ejaculation is more likely to occur if the male is anxious or if there is a lack of privacy, such as in a parked car. It is particularly likely to occur during first intercourse when the male is in a state of high sexual excitement. Many males are disappointed with their first sexual experience because they achieved orgasm more quickly than they would have preferred.

Impotency is the inability to achieve or maintain an erection sufficient to perform intercourse. There are many possible causes for impotency, including anxiety, guilt feelings or concern one's partner is judging his performance especially if she is more sexually experienced than he is. Physical factors such as alcohol and fatigue and certain health conditions can also bring on impotency.

Among young women a common sexual concern is the inability to achieve orgasm through intercourse. Hass (1979) found that only 6% of sexually active teenage girls reported achieving orgasm every time they had intercourse and one-third were not sure if they had ever experienced an orgasm. Major factors inhibiting orgasm were: not wanting to have sex but doing so because of the partner's wishes, not being totally relaxed, not being emotionally involved with the partner, guilt feelings, fear of pregnancy, lack of sufficient sexual stimulation, and an inexperienced or insensitive partner.

In a questionnaire survey of 105 university females who were sexually experienced, I found that one-half said they could achieve orgasm during intercourse without additional clitoral stimulation. One-third could achieve orgasm during intercourse only if they had additional clitoral stimulation and 16% could not achieve orgasm during intercourse. About half of the women said they sometimes used additional clitoral stimulation during intercourse to achieve orgasm. Because women may believe there is something wrong with them if they cannot achieve orgasm during intercourse, it is important they be informed that this is common and that they are not abnormal if they do not experience orgasm during intercourse. Sex educators could relieve a tremendous amount of sexual anxiety by making this fact known.

When we have intercourse I try to pretend that I enjoyed it as much as he did, for fear that he would think me as being frigid. I was never able to communicate my needs or how he should please me because of my embarrassment for needing clitoral stimulation and because he might take it as an attack on his ability as a lover.

There is considerable variation among women in the ability to achieve orgasm. Some achieve orgasm quickly and easily while others require a lengthy period of clitoral stimulation. In my study 8% reported they could achieve orgasm through fantasy alone without additional physical stimulation. Seventeen percent reported achieving orgasm through breast stimulation alone. On the other hand, 5% reported they were non-orgasmic.

In our achievement oriented society there is considerable pressure to be a "good lover". Many women worry about whether their sexual performance is pleasing to the male. Unfortunately many young people believe that the ideal female sex partner is one who obtains orgasms easily with little stimulation. Some males define a woman as being abnormal or frigid if she doesn't have an orgasm during intercourse. Because of the influence of the media, some males expect that all women should have intense multiple orgasms and when they don't they are disappointed.

The following quotes given by university women illustrate some of the problems encountered because of unrealistic expectations regarding female sexual response:

I had such high expectations that nothing could have lived up to them. This had led to the feeling that there was something wrong or why wouldn't I be getting more pleasure out of sex all the time and why wasn't sex perfect every time.

Since I had experienced orgasm from masturbation, I assumed I would in intercourse and that the whole activity would be even more pleasurable. Physically, the experience was a disappointment. However, the closeness and warmth I experienced made it gratifying emotionally.

I could achieve orgasm only through direct, manual or oral clitoral stimulation. This made me feel rather inadequate and I began to wonder if I might be frigid. I can enjoy the closeness of the sex act and be satisfied without achieving orgasm but I fell into the old trap of thinking that it was necessary to achieve orgasm through intercourse to be completely satisfied sexually.

Because my partner and I were both of the impression that female orgasm should occur through penile-vaginal intercourse, when I was unable to reach orgasm certain feelings of inadequacy were experienced by both of us, placing a strain on our relationship. My feelings of incompetence grew as the relationship progressed and I was unable to reach orgasm. Sex became for me an activity in which my actual 'femaleness' was challenged.

After my partner obtained orgasm, he was not concerned whether I had an orgasm or not. Later, he attributed my 'failure' to reach orgasm as my 'holding back'.

My boyfriend thought there must be something wrong with me since we had had intercourse many times and I had never had an orgasm. Since he did not know that I masturbated to orgasm, he began to regard me as abnormal and perhaps even 'frigid'. My boyfriend's expectations made me feel guilty that I didn't have orgasms during intercourse. I began to tell him just exactly how I did and didn't want to be touched. The effect of this was that he thought I should be even more likely to have an orgasm since he was giving me the kind of stimulation I needed. By this time, I felt I had been cast into a stereotype of being non-orgasmic and I found it difficult to let him know otherwise. One reason for this probably was that I was afraid I would insult his masculinity by telling him I could have an orgasm by myself. Also I resented his expectations and felt he wanted me to have an orgasm just to prove he was a good lover.

One of the mistaken assumptions about sexuality is that sexual pleasure should come naturally. In fact, many young people are disappointed because they do not experience in their sexual relations the pleasurable fantasies which they had anticipated. Younger teenage girls in particular are likely to report that they do not enjoy sex. Many of these girls are engaging in sexual relations because they feel that they might lose their boyfriends if they did not engage in sex. For many young women, enjoyment of sex is something that has to be learned over time. However, many mistakenly assume that they are frigid because they are not achieving the sexual peaks which they have assumed they would.

A different problem faced by some young people is that they have been conditioned into being repulsed by sex. Those raised by extremely punitive and moralistic parents may develop the attitude that sex is disgusting and degrading. They might have been discovered by their parents in such sexual activities as "playing doctor" or masturbation and were subjected to harsh punishment and made to feel they committed a terrible sin. This causes them to repress any sexual feelings and to develop tremendous guilt feelings whenever they have sexual thoughts.

After wondering about each other's bodies and the differences between a girl and a boy, my cousin (male) and I locked ourselves in the bathroom and exposed our bodies. We were interrupted by our parents. We were both spanked and sent to bed immediately. This led me to believe that sex was something terrible.

Others develop a negative image of sex after being molested by a relative or other adults.

One of the common questions young people have about their sexuality is "Am I normal?" Despite the apparent openness surrounding sexuality, there is still a great deal of secrecy. Young people are often unaware of what others are doing sexually and this results in pluralistic ignorance where people are engaging in a particular sexual practice but believe they are the only ones doing it. Because of this situation, adolescents are very interested in statistics regarding current sexual practices. They want to find if they fall in the majority or the minority group. If they fall within the majority group, there is a feeling of relief. If, on the other hand, they fall within the minority group, they tend to either feel somewhat uneasy or else to reject the statistics.

When an area of one's life such as sex is considered to be secretive, it often assumes exaggerated proportions resulting in anxiety and a concern over normality. Young people often worry that their involvement in sexual behaviours such as masturbation or oral sex might be viewed by others as perversion. Thus they look to statistics to reaffirm their feelings of normality. In the absence of clearly defined societal norms, it is not surprising that the statistical norm has come to replace the value norm as a criterion for normality.

Two university women stated:

I felt very ashamed and abnormal for thinking about sex and having to masturbate. None of my friends ever talked about such things and I doubted that they were going through the same turmoil.

It is a relief to find out that our sexual behaviour is not much different from others when originally you thought your feelings and behaviour were abnormal. It is odd how in sexual matters there tends to be a feeling of isolation as though you were the only person to feel a certain way.

Because in our society there are such negative sanctions associated with being sexually different from others, people present a sexual image of themselves which they believe will conform to the expectations of others. For example, if an adolescent female with liberal sexual attitudes should meet a conservative female, she would be unlikely to disclose her real attitudes. On the other hand, if she should perceive that the other woman also has liberal attitudes, then she is more likely to be open about her true feelings regarding sex. The same type of process occurs when friends are discussing their sexual experiences. It is rare that one will be completely open about her sexual experiences without knowing the sexual experiences of the others or that the others would be accepting of her behaviour. Young people are very cautious about revealing themselves because they fear that if their sexual behaviour is exposed it might be ridiculed or condemned by others.

Promiscuity

The label of promiscuity reflects a continuing double standard. One indication of society's negative attitude regarding casual sexuality among women is the fact that words such as "slut" are used to condemn women but not men. The woman with many sexual partners is generally viewed as having emotional problems whereas the male with many sexual partners is likely to be viewed as a normal male and perhaps even be admired for his successful "conquests". Whereas a young woman who is considered promiscuous might be referred to a professional for counselling, this seldom happens to a male because this would not be defined as a problem. The common stereotype of the woman with multiple partners is that she is suffering from low self-esteem and other psychological problems which are driving her to promiscuity. Again, this explanation is seldom given for males.

Even in today's permissive society, most young women are concerned about the possibility of being labelled as promiscuous. There is often the fear among young women that their sexual partner might disclose their sexual activity resulting in public ridicule for her. Women try to avoid the promiscuous label by only engaging in premarital intercourse within a love relationship because they believe that being in love makes sex moral, so then they cannot be defined as promiscuous. Another strategy is to avoid having intercourse with males who might talk about their sexual activity.

There are other problems with casual relationships in addition to acquiring a "bad" reputation. Some people cannot respond sexually unless they feel they can trust the other person. Also in a casual relationship one is more reluctant to state one's sexual preferences and needs. Another danger of casual sex is the increased risk of contracting a venereal disease and there is particular concern today about the genital herpes virus. Many young women feel guilty if they engage in casual sex.

A university female commented:

At one point I thought that maybe I should be daring and try casual sex. I'd seen my friends engaging in it and enjoying it, so I thought why not give it a try. The few times I tried it, I was left with a lot of sex guilt. I enjoyed myself at the time, but afterwards I felt really dissatisfied with and uncomfortable about the whole situation. For me sex is part of a committed relationship.

However, some people seem to be able to handle casual sexual encounters without serious difficulty. These people typically view sex as recreational activity not requiring heavy emotional involvement.

One 19-year-old university female stated:

I have a very strong sex drive and I enjoy having sex with different men. This doesn't bother my friends because I only choose friends who can accept my sexual behaviour. If other people reject me because of my sexual belief, then I consider it their problem and not mine.

Some young people may prefer sex within a love relationship but may try casual sex to relieve sexual frustration.

Being unsuccessful in finding someone with whom to be involved in a steady relationship, my options were either to abstain from sex or change my sexual values. As I realized that I missed having my physical needs met, my values changed from permissiveness with affection to that of a hedonistic nature—"if it feels good, do it". My peers gave support to my new values and behaviour as many of my girlfriends were in similar situations of not having boyfriends and yet wanting to fulfill sexual drives.

Physical Problems

Many adolescent females anticipate there will be physical pain at first intercourse. Because of this fear, first intercourse is often unpleasurable for the female. In one study I found that 50% of females experienced pain at first intercourse. Anxiety over the fear of pain can result in vaginismus or the tightening of the muscles at the vaginal opening resulting in serious discomfort when the male attempts penetration.

Vaginal infections are common among sexually active young women. However, young women may not recognize the symptoms or else they will put up with uncomfortable symptoms because they are too embarrassed to see a physician. Often they will put up with painful intercourse because they believe that the problem is psychological.

Physicians are becoming concerned about the increased medical consequences of early sexual activity. In addition to pregnancy and sexually transmitted diseases, physicians are concerned about the increased risk of cancer of the cervix and sterility resulting from vaginal infections, particularly among those beginning sexual relations at an early age.

Males are also at risk of contracting sexually transmitted diseases, particularly as a consequence of sexual relations with multiple part-ners. Few males experience pain at first intercourse, however males who have not been circumcised and have a tight foreskin may ex-perience some pain during intercourse when the foreskin is retracted.

Another problem is the fear that one's physical development is abnormal. Many young people have fears that their genitals are ab-normal. For example, some young women worry that the labia minora are too big. It is important that physicians performing examinations on young people anticipate these concerns and provide reassurance that "things" are normal. Some physicians will provide a hand mirror during the internal examination so that the woman can learn about her own body.

A university female commented:

> *Just before my first year of university I was sure that I had some sort of cancerous growth in my genital area. I finally went to a female doctor during my first year only to find that it was the labia which had developed to be quite large but not beyond the bounds of "normal". I thanked the doctor and apologized for my lack of education.*

Another woman who was also concerned her genitals were abnor-mal commented:

> *After the doctor examined me he erased any feelings of my being physically abnormal, by telling me that everything looked perfectly normal and perfectly female.*

Sexuality and Disability

While many young people have difficulties in adjusting to their sexual development, those with physical or mental handicaps face even greater difficulties. Although the physically disabled have different types of problems than those who are mentally disabled, they face similar types of sexual discrimination and prejudices. Because of their disa-bilities they are often viewed by others as being less than complete human beings. When people become preoccupied with the disability itself, the other human needs of the disabled are frequently neglected. Sexuality is a prime example of this as there is a common stereotype that disabled people do not have sexual desires and therefore do not need to have sex education.

In a study of 47 physically disabled young people in Calgary, many of the young people reported they had not received adequate sex education and one-half thought their parents were trying to protect them from having to deal with their sexuality (Robinson, 1980). Two-thirds thought their physical disability made it more difficult to establish a sexual relationship with a partner. Lacking self-confidence about their ability to attract someone of the opposite sex, many were highly sensitive to the possibility of being rejected. Yet almost all of the young people agreed they should be provided with the opportunity of having social and physical relationships in privacy.

The mentally disabled may even face more serious sexual discrimination than the physically disabled. Because the mentally disabled are often viewed as being childlike, caregivers believe that they should be "protected" against possible sexual dangers. Any sex education that is provided seldom goes beyond the most elementary reproductive facts. In institutions the sexes are often segregated and only allowed to interact under supervision on special occasions. Restricted access to heterosexual activity may encourage an increase in masturbation and/or homosexual behaviour. When these behaviours occur, they are often dealt with inappropriately by staff members. Not only are the mentally disabled confused about what is sexually permissible, but the caregivers are often themselves unsure as to what should be considered inappropriate behaviour. One rationale given by caregivers for the close supervision of the mentally disabled is the fear that the mentally disabled might be subject to sexual victimization. Rather than preparing the young disabled person to deal with the possibility of sexual exploitation, close supervision of his behaviour is given instead.

The major sexual concern regarding the mentally handicapped is that of unwanted pregnancies. While there is continuing debate over the issues of providing birth control devices and sterilization, little research has been done regarding the ability of the sexually active mentally disabled to successfully use contraception. In the meantime, with deinstitutionalization of the mentally disabled, there will be an increasing need to provide those living in the community with adequate sex education so that they can have the resources to make more informed decisions regarding sexuality and parenthood.

Sexual Offenses Against Females

Today there is increasing interest in the topic of sexual offenses against women. A weakness of most studies of sexual assault is that they focus on reported cases rather than unreported ones. This is a serious deficiency because most sexual offenses are unreported. Previous victimology research has focused on the most serious assaults such as rape; therefore, we lack knowledge about other types of sexual offenses such as being sexually molested, exhibitionism, obscene phone calls, and being followed.

In studying sexual offenses, we conducted a questionnaire survey among 103 university females from two university classes (Herold, Mantle & Zemitis, 1979). When respondents were asked how much they worried about sexual offenses or assaults occurring to them, only 18% said they never worried about this. Most said that they were either slightly (46%) or moderately (29%) worried while 7% said they were very worried. Eighty-four percent of the subjects reported having been the victim of at least one sexual offense. Twenty-five percent had experienced one of these offenses while 42% had experienced two or three of the offenses.

Nine percent reported having experienced attempted rape or other sexual assaults before the age of 14, and 16% had been exposed to an exhibitionist. The most common sexual offense after age 14 was being sexually molested, with 44% of the respondents indicating this had happened to them. The least prevalent type of sexual offense was rape, with one person reporting this.

Of those reporting sexual offenses, most said it occurred once. For example, 69% of those reporting attempted rape and 60% of those reporting seeing an exhibitionist, said it happened once. Also the one person who reported having been raped said this happened once. Being sexually molested occurred more frequently with 57% of these victims reporting such an incident occurring two or three times.

A sexual offense can severely disrupt one's normal pattern of living and bring about crisis reactions. In particular it can bring about the feeling that one has lost control of one's life. One of the worst problems is the unpredictability of not knowing whether or not the sexual offense may recur. The most serious assaults can affect functioning in almost all areas of one's life. With rape victims this is referred to as the "rape trauma syndrome" which can involve such symptoms as having recurring nightmares of the rape, developing a general fear of men, finding it difficult to work and being unable to enjoy sexual relations. This reaction is illustrated in the following case:

> *One time when I was 11, I was staying at my uncle's. He sat me on his lap and proceeded to fondle my breasts which I found disgusting. He*

continued to make passes at me whenever I went to visit, that's when I told my parents. I have never seen him since. He made me scared of men and for a long time I was afraid to be left alone with any man no matter who he was.

When respondents were asked to indicate how affected they were by the sexual offenses, they indicated extreme upset to attempted rape, moderate upset to sexual molestation, and slight to moderate upset in response to seeing an exhibitionist (see Table 2). Sixty-three percent of attempted rape victims had been extremely upset compared with 27% of those who had been sexually molested and 11% who had seen an exhibitionist.

Most victims of attempted rape (59%) and of exhibitionism (84%) were assaulted by a complete stranger, whereas this was true for only 24% who had been sexually molested (see Table 3). About one-half of those who had been sexually molested indicated that the offender was either an acquaintance or a casual date. Other offenders listed were neighbour, friend of victim's parents, girlfriend's brother and physician. The one person who had been raped indicated that the offender was a complete stranger.

Most victims of sexual offenses find it helpful to discuss what happened with someone they can trust and who can provide support and comfort. Almost all of the attempted rape victims (94%), most of the exhibitionist victims (71%) and about one-half (57%) of sexually molested victims had told someone of the incident, usually a friend. Few victims reported sexual offenses to either relatives, police or health or social work professionals. Sixteen percent of attempted rape victims reported to police and only 8% discussed the incident with a professional. Of the exhibitionist victims, only 4% reported the event to police and none discussed it with a professional person. Of those

TABLE 2
EMOTIONAL RESPONSE OF VICTIMS OF SEXUAL OFFENSE

Degree of Emotion Expressed	Attempted Rape (N = 16) %	Exhibitionist (N = 28) %	Sexually Molested (N = 37) %
Not upset	0	21	0
Slightly upset	6	33	24
Moderately upset	31	35	49
Extremely upset	63	11	27
Total	100	100	100

TABLE 3
RELATIONSHIP OF VICTIM TO OFFENDER

Relationship of Victim to Offender	Attempted Rape (N = 16) %	Exhibitionist (N = 28) %	Sexually Molested (N = 37) %
Complete stranger	59	84	24
Known by sight	0	3	9
Acquaintance	17	3	36
Relative	0	7	4
Friend	0	3	6
Steady boyfriend	0	0	2
Casual date	6	0	16
Other	18	0	3
Total	100	100	100

who had been sexually molested, none reported this to either police or a professional person. Victims give the following reasons for not reporting sexual offenses: they believe it is a private matter, they believe the offender will not be punished, they believe the police may not be willing to prosecute, or worse, they fear that the police might embarrass or humiliate them by their questioning, and finally the victim might fear reprisal (Black, 1974). Furthermore some women attribute blame to themselves and feel that they are somewhat responsible for the offense. The fact that only a small percentage of sexual offenses are reported and that offenses of greater physical severity are more likely to be reported obviously alters the composition of offenses documented in police records.

The most common sexual offense is the obscene phone call with 61% having received obscene phone calls. Of these, 27% reported this had happened once, 57% reported two to four times, and 16% reported five or more times. Only 7% contacted the telephone company concerning the obscene phone calls and even fewer (3%) reported this to the police. Although this offense can cause great emotional distress in the victim, there has been a lack of research into this problem area. Perhaps, because the offense is verbal rather than physical, it is not considered a serious problem by law enforcement officials. Despite the development of sophisticated tracing equipment, telephone companies are reluctant to become involved in attempting to trace obscene phone calls because of the financial cost involved. Even though victims might find these calls to be emotionally disturbing and traumatic, neither the telephone company or the police are likely to be sympathetic or helpful. They will generally intervene only if the phone calls persist on a regular basis over a lengthy period of time or if they become life-threatening.

Another type of sexual offense which can be not only bothersome but also unnerving is that of being followed on the street. In this situation women are anxious about the possible intentions of the male who is following and are concerned that an attack might occur. When asked about whether they had ever been followed for the purpose of sexual harassment, 24% of the respondents indicated they had. Most sexual offenses are committed by males against females. However, along with the increased sexual liberation of women has also come an apparent increase in the number of sexual offenses committed by women. Because it is more common today for women to take the sexual initiative, there is an increased probability of their offending others. Eight respondents indicated that they had been sexually propositioned by another female and of these, five indicated they were moderately to extremely offended.

Sexual offenses, particularly those involving physical contact, can seriously affect one's normal sexual relationships. If the woman is sexually inexperienced, the offense may make her extremely negative regarding sex and make it difficult for her to later establish a satisfying sexual relationship. A woman involved in an on-going sexual relationship may now find it difficult to respond sexually after a sexual assault. She may also want to avoid sexual practices which were forced upon her by the rapist even though she may have previously enjoyed these with her partner (Burgess and Holmstrom, 1979).

Twenty-four percent of the respondents indicated that the sexual offense(s) made them feel more negative about sex. Almost one-half agreed that the sexual offense(s) resulted in a fear of males. Nearly all of the respondents (98%) indicated that they did not believe that they contributed to any of the sexual offenses that had happened to them.

Accompanying changes in sexual attitudes have been changes in sexual offense patterns. In the 1950's a study of sexual offenses against university women (Kirkpatrick & Kanin, 1957) found that sexual offenses such as attempted rape were more likely to occur at the "going steady" phase of a dating relationship. This is not surprising when we consider the fact that at that time males accepted the standard of sex in a steady dating relationship but far fewer women did. Today, however, when sexual offenses occur in the dating context, they are more likely to occur at the casual dating stage. This is because there is little difference between males and females in terms of acceptance of sexual activity in a committed dating type of relationship, but there is still a considerable difference between the sexes in acceptance of premarital sex at the casual dating phase. Consequently, males today expect sexual activity to occur at an earlier phase in a dating relationship than did males twenty years ago.

Sexual Decision-Making

Conflicting standards for sexual behaviour have made the process of sexual decision-making very difficult and can cause considerable conflict in a relationship.

Until we finally decided that we'd have premarital sex our relationship was always on and off and we fought about whether we should have sex or not. Our whole relationship seemed to be around yes or no. Once we decided this, we could relate to each other on an easier basis and talk about a lot more things because we had one part of it settled that seemed to be causing so much upset.

I know he wants me to have sex with him and I am worried because I want to as well. I feel so bad just thinking about it. I mean I am a Catholic. I am not supposed to have sex before marriage. I don't see why I shouldn't and yet I know later I'd feel really guilty.

The young woman is still expected to play the gatekeeper role of deciding how far sexual behaviour should proceed, so the burden of decision-making is placed primarily on her. It is up to her to decide whether or not to engage in sexual relations with a particular partner and if so at what stage in the relationship. If she decides to permit sexual relations early in the relationship, then she has the worry that her partner may decide she is too "easy" and may dislike her because of this. However, if she prohibits sexual activity for a lengthy time, she may worry about losing her partner to someone else who is more accommodating.

When I was in high school I did not date very much. Although morally I felt that petting was wrong, I allowed my dating partner to pet with me because I wanted to be popular. I did not enjoy it but I felt it was necessary in order to be able to date.

I wondered if something was wrong with me because I didn't feel like having sex. What if I never became interested? I began to worry that I may never keep a male's interest because I would not have intercourse. I began to think I really had nothing worthwhile to offer a male except my sexuality. At the age of seventeen I found I could not keep a man interested in me for any considerable length of time unless I was prepared to sleep with him. Anger and hurt, plus disbelief in my inadequacy, damaged my self-image.

Although I enjoyed the closeness of our sexual encounters and was just as easily aroused as he was I was uncomfortable with the idea of having sexual relations. That I continued to engage in such behaviour indicates my need, at the time, for the emotional support and my fear of losing my only boyfriend to date. The conflict between my attitude and behaviour was a potent source of guilt feelings.

Disagreements can occur not only with respect to sexual intercourse but also over other sexual activities. For example, given the increase in oral sex, couples may disagree about whether or not to participate in oral sex. One high school female stated:

Disagreement about oral-genital sex is a major problem in our relationship. I think it is dirty and my boyfriend doesn't, so he gets upset when I don't want to do it.

Decision-making is also problematic because many young people cannot openly communicate about sexuality and find it difficult to let each other know what their real feelings and desires are. There is the fear that if they say the wrong thing they might offend the partner so instead they try to play it safe by not being honest.

Although I was able to express interest in sex, I was not able to be open with my sex needs. I could not admit that I needed to have an orgasm after my first intercourse experience, so I could not bring myself to masturbate in front of my boyfriend or ask him to masturbate me.

Admittedly, changes in sexual behaviour among young people have resulted in an increased number of sexual problems. On the other hand, young people today are more accepting of their sexuality and their sexual needs. Yet, we must also recognize that many young people have not experienced sexual intercourse. Because of this, the discussion of sexuality among young people must be placed in a balanced perspective.

Also, for those who are sexually experienced, it should be noted that sex is only one part of their relationship, and it is usually secondary to the emotional aspects. As one woman stated:

For me the most important part of our sexual relationship is the emotional closeness I feel with my partner. Sex is for us a mutual expression of emotional feeling.

Theories of Premarital Sexuality

Several different explanations and/or theories have been used to explain the increase in sexual behaviour among young people. Often single causes are given such as: the breakdown of the family, the influence of the mass media and the Women's Liberation Movement. A widely held belief is that the birth control pill is solely responsible for changes in sexual behaviour. While the pill may have some influence on sexual permissiveness by taking away the worry about pregnancy, its influence on promoting sexual behaviour has been overstated. For example, in our research we have found that fewer than 20% of adolescents begin taking the birth control pill before first having intercourse. Many wait for six months or longer after beginning intercourse before they begin taking the pill (Herold & Goodwin, 1980). Rather than stimulating sexual behaviour, the pill is usually a consequence of increased sexual activity occurring on a regular basis. Nevertheless, there is no question that the pill has had a dramatic effect on the prevention of unwanted pregnancies among sexually active young women.

Researchers studying premarital sexuality have developed different theories to explain why some young people engage in premarital sexual behaviour and others do not. The major theoretical approaches will be presented in this chapter.

Biological Theory

Genetic and hormonal factors may account for some sexual behaviour differences. Kinsey et al. (1953) suggested that differences in sexual behaviour of adolescent boys and girls could be partially explained by the higher androgen levels in teenage boys that in teenage girls. Also, as the level of androgen hormones in males decreases over the life cycle, there is an accompanying decrease in the strength of the sex drive among males.

A biological factor which may account for sexual differences among females is the age of menarche. The average age at menarche declined from 13.5 in 1940 to 12.5 in 1968 (Freeman & Rickels, 1979). According to this menstruation theory, teenage girls are engaging in sexual activity at younger ages today because they are menstruating at younger ages. In one study it was found that teenage girls who menstruated at younger ages were more likely to engage in intercourse at younger ages (Zabin et al., 1979). Perhaps girls who mature earlier have a stronger sex drive. As well, girls who mature physically at an earlier age attract male attention and are more likely to be asked for dates at a young age.

Included under biological theories is the factor of physical attractiveness. Our society heavily emphasizes the importance of physical attractiveness, especially for women. Physically attractive individuals are more appealing to the opposite sex and thus are more likely to be involved in a dating relationship and have more opportunity for sexual involvement. Perlman (1978), in a study of Manitoba university students, found that for females but not males being physically attractive was associated with: greater participation in dating, more permissive attitudes toward premarital sex and a higher number of coital partners.

Cultural Theory

Sexual behaviour can arouse strong negative emotions and has the potential to cause serious interpersonal conflict. Thus some sexual control is found in every society in order to prevent the disruption of social relationships. Sexual behaviour is controlled by emotional conditioning of the individual so that he regulates his own behaviour and feels guilty if he violates the sexual norm. Control is also enforced by others through such means as gossip and public ridicule. There is also the situational control exercised by parents and other authorities who may so closely regulate the behaviour of young people that there is no opportunity for them to be alone in situations where intercourse might occur.

Repressive social control of sex reached its zenith during the Victorian era when a good woman was not supposed to have any interest in sex or to derive any enjoyment from it. Sex was for purely procreative reasons and a woman submitted to her husband's advances as part of her wifely duty. Victorian morality held steadfast until World War I, which disrupted many of the traditional social controls and facilitated the more permissive atmosphere of the 1920's.

A basic assumption of cultural theory is that sexual behaviour is affected by cultural conditioning. Thus the rate of premarital sex is higher in Sweden, where there is greater acceptance of premarital sex than in Moslem societies such as Pakistan where it is not accepted. In North America sexual behaviour has changed in response to societal values emphasizing personal fulfillment and gratification as opposed to self-restraint. Because societies are usually more concerned about controlling the sexual behaviour of females than of males, the effect of negative cultural conditioning is seen more often in women than in men. Kinsey (1953) emphasized this point in his finding that sexual arousal and activity among adolescent females was lower than for women in their late thirties and early forties. Kinsey believed that because of this negative sexual conditioning, it took most women several years to rid themselves of negative views toward sex. Kinsey's studies were conducted at a time when North American society strongly disapproved of premarital sex. Given the greater sexual freedom of young women today, it is questionable whether his generalization regarding the age at which women reach the peak of their sexuality would still be true. Further research is needed to answer this question.

The role of culture is also seen in the effect of social class on sexual behaviour. Kinsey found that lower class males began having intercourse at younger ages than middle or upper class males. A more recent American study (Tavris and Sadd, 1975) found that women with less than high school education experienced intercourse at an average age of 16 compared to age 18 for college graduates. In a study of high school students in Calgary, intercourse experience was higher among those from lower social class backgrounds (Meikle et al., 1981). Thus, it appears young people who plan to go to college are more likely to delay having intercourse than those who do not complete high school.

Reference Group Theory

One of the major sociological approaches used to explain premarital sexual behaviour is reference group theory. The reference group provides the individual with normative standards to use in decision-making. Merton (1957) delineated normative and comparative reference groups. The normative reference group sets standards for the individual and the comparison reference group provides a basis of comparison by which the individual can evaluate himself and others. However, the same reference can serve both functions. For example, an adolescent might perceive his friends as both accepting of premarital sex (normative reference group) and also as engaging in premarital sex (comparative reference group). During adolescence the peer group and dating partner become more significant reference groups than parents. Generally, peer groups are more permissive than parents; however, there still are conservative peer groups, particularly the more religious, which do support parental norms.

Ira Reiss (1967), a theorist in premarital sexual research, has integrated cultural and reference group explanations for interpreting differing rates of premarital sexual activity. One of the key propositions which he has formulated still forms a basis for much of the theoretical explanation of premarital sex. This proposition states:

> *The degree of acceptable premarital sexual permissiveness in a courtship group varies directly with the degree of autonomy of the courtship group and with the degree of acceptable premarital sexual permissiveness in the social and cultural setting outside the group.*
>
> (Reiss, 1967, p. 167)

For example, if a dating couple is not closely supervised by parents and if their peer group approves of premarital sex, then that couple is likely to have premarital sex.

Deviance Theory

Premarital sex has traditionally been defined as deviant behaviour because it has been disapproved of by many people in our society.

Given the greater acceptability of premarital sex today, it is question-able whether or not premarital sex especially among adolescents 18 or 19 years of age can truly be considered deviant behaviour, partic-ularly if it occurs within the commonly accepted standard among adolescents of love with affection. However, the situation is different for younger teenagers who still are considered not mature enough to be responsible about their sexual behaviour. Few adolescents expe-rience sexual intercourse before the age of 15 and most adolescents themselves consider it inappropriate to engage in premarital sex at a young age. Those who engage in premarital intercourse during the younger teenage years are clearly departing from accepted behaviour for that age group. Not surprisingly, research studies have found that adolescents who engage in premarital intercourse during their early teenage years are likely to belong to a delinquent subcultural group (Jessor & Jessor, 1975). Hundleby (1979), in a study of grade 9 and 10 students in Ontario, found the boys and girls who had engaged in premarital intercourse were also likely to have engaged in delin-quent activities such as stealing and vandalism and were more likely to have used tobacco and alcohol than others of their age group.

According to deviance theory, the sexual behaviour of this younger group would be explained as being part of their overall rejection of societal norms. The same factors which lead them to engage in criminal behaviour also lead them to engage in sexual behaviour.

Opportunity Theory

Another explanation for increased sexual activity among teenagers is that there is greater opportunity. Much of teenage sexual activity can occur in the parental home during the daytime when both parents are working or when parents are away on holidays or out for an evening. Obviously in situations where a parent is not working and is home all day, this is unlikely to occur.

With increasing mobility and urban anonymity, social controls over sexual behaviour have been reduced so that it is possible for teenagers of the opposite sex to spend the afternoon in the parental home without any of the neighbours taking an interest in them. This would have been unheard of a few years ago and would have provoked considerable gossip in the community. Today the chances are that the neighbours are also away at work.

Increased freedom for young people is also seen in university res-idences where there are no longer restrictions on visits by the opposite sex. Until the middle 1960's colleges and universities had dormitory regulations relating to standards of sexual conduct for students, but hardly any have these today. While in the late 1960's there was controversy about whether or not a female student should be allowed to have a male visitor in her dormitory room, this is no longer considered an issue. This change occurred during the late 1960's and early 1970's when there was considerable student pressure put on universities to relinquish the role of surrogate parent.

The most immediate environmental change that I experienced upon arriving at university was the total absence of parental control, and for that matter, any adult supervision. This, combined with the complete privacy that my own room afforded us, added an element of security and safety to our sexual relationship that had previously been threatened by fear of discovery.

Largely as a result of student pressure, college health services began providing contraceptives for students. Today many universities openly advertise their birth control services with the belief that providing contraceptive services should be included in the general health care program for students.

Personality Theory

Until recently a common assumption among psychiatrists was that young people engaged in premarital sexual behaviour because of personality problems and deficiencies. It was hypothesized that persons with low self-esteem were likely to engage in premarital sex in order to secure love or to feel more accepted.

Stratton and Spitzer (1967) hypothesized that the relationship between self-esteem and sexual permissiveness is dependent upon societal norms. At a conservative college where most students disapproved of premarital intercourse, Stratton and Spitzer found that students who deviated from this norm by approving of premarital intercourse had lower self-esteem. Perlman (1974), on the other hand, found with a sample of students at a moderately permissive university that there was no association between esteem and permissiveness. Perlman's findings suggest that if society approves of premarital sex, then persons with high self-esteem are as likely to engage in sex as those with low self-esteem. However, those with high self-esteem are less likely to engage in premarital sex if they do not want to, whereas low self-esteem persons may do so because they fear being rejected. High esteem women are also more experienced in their sex lives and more willing to try different sexual techniques and activities (Maslow, 1942).

In our study of young women attending birth control clinics, we found that young women with high self-esteem were more likely to accept premarital sex in a love relationship than those having low self-esteem. High-esteem women had less sexual guilt and were more likely to believe that single women should be able to make the first move in sexual relations with men. However, there was no relationship between self-esteem and the acceptance of premarital intercourse without affection or the number of coital partners. Although high-esteem women were more accepting of premarital intercourse in a love relationship, they were not more accepting of casual sex than women with low self-esteem.

Of the personality variables, sexual guilt has the strongest relationship with premarital permissiveness. High sex guilt students have more restrictive attitudes toward premarital sex and have less sexual experience than low sex guilt students (Mosher & Cross, 1971).

Eysenck (1976) reports that extroverts are more likely to engage in premarital sexual activity and have premartial sex more frequently. He argues that this is because extroverts are more sociable, impulsive and active.

Exchange Theory

The main premise of exchange theory is that each person seeks to maximize his rewards and to minimize his costs. The exchange theory perspective of premarital sex is that women have a scarce resource which men desire, namely, sexual favours. In order to minimize their costs women are selective in granting their sexual favours because a potential cost of providing sex is the loss of reputation.

In our society sex is often viewed as a gift or reward that women give to men or that men take by force. Sex is not seen as something that men have to offer women. It is up to the female to decide whether or not she wants to grant sexual favours to the male and it is also up to her to decide how far sexual relations will go. This theory accounts for why it is that females have the gatekeeper role of determining how far sexual activity will go. The theory also offers insight into the stereotypes of male and female sexuality, namely, that men are out to get all they can sexually and that women don't enjoy sex but instead engage in sexual relations to please a male who in turn will offer love and affection or at least material benefits.

In addition to the actual physical pleasure received in a sexual relationship, a significant benefit for some males is being able to tell their friends about the sexual experience. In many peer groups men can achieve considerable prestige in being able to relate details of the latest sexual conquest. Carns (1973), in a study of male-female differences in communication about sexual behaviour found that after first intercourse women tended to wait longer than males to tell any of their friends about the experience. However, in a situation where the male cares about and is in love with his sexual partner, he is less likely to disclose the details of that sexual relationship.

One of the basic assumptions of exchange theory is that exchange processes create a differentiation of power. This is clearly shown in the case of Waller's (1937) "principle of least interest" which states that the person who is least interested in maintaining a relationship has control of that relationship. That person has the better bargaining position because he or she is not as likely to give concessions as is the individual who is more interested in maintaining the relationship. If one person does control the relationship, exploitation is often the result. Waller found that some students would often try to get their dating partners to become emotionally committed so that they could control the relationship. Women would exploit to obtain presents and expensive amusements, while the male exploiter would seek sexual gains.

Finally, the exchange theory explanation for the increase in premarital sexual behaviour especially among women is that sexual intercourse has become less costly and more rewarding. In the 1940's losing virginity was considered a fate worse than death. Today not only is it more socially acceptable to have premarital intercourse, but women are expected to have the right to sexual pleasure. Also, with the birth control pill there is less risk of pregnancy.

This theory may also explain why fewer young people are married today than in previous years. When young people were less likely to experience premarital sex, there was a greater incentive to marry to obtain sexual fulfillment. Because today it is easier for young people to have sexual relations, there is less incentive to get married for sexual reasons.

The Transition From Virginity to Non-Virginity

Most researchers have analyzed virgins and nonvirgins as discrete entities. However, there are important subclassifications. In particular, D'Augelli and Cross (1975) identified adamant virgins and potential nonvirgins and found that adamant virgins believed intercourse should be saved for marriage and were strongly influenced by parents and religion, whereas potential nonvirgins believed that given the right situation and the right person they would have intercourse.

In the early 1960's greater inconsistencies in sexual attitudes and behaviour were found among nonvirgins than among virgins. Given general disapproval of premarital sex, many nonvirgins engaged in intercourse before personally accepting the idea of having premarital intercourse. In other words, sexual behaviour preceded changes in sexual standards.

Today, given the greater acceptability of premarital intercourse, there are fewer regretful nonvirgins and more women who approve of intercourse but have not yet engaged in it. In a study of women at the University of Manitoba, Perlman (1978) found that many were virgins who approved of premarital intercourse in a love relationship. Of these virgins one-half had never been involved in a love relationship and Perlman suggests that the absence of an appropriate partner may explain why these women have not had intercourse. Jessor and Jessor (1975) in a longitudinal study used the concept of transition-proneness to differentiate virgins who became sexually active from virgins who maintained their virginity. Their major hypothesis was that there were differences between virgins and potential nonvirgins (transition group) prior to the shift from virginity to nonvirginity and that these differences could serve to signal the onset of nonvirginity.

By comparing the transitional group of potential nonvirgins with both adamant virgins and nonvirgins, we can come to a better understanding of the interaction of sexual attitudes and behaviour. The potential nonvirgins are a useful group for analysis because they have the same attitudinal acceptance of premarital intercourse as do the nonvirgins but behaviourally they are in the same category as the adamant virgins.

Using the student study data (Herold and Goodwin, 1981) we analyzed factors which might help us to understand the cognitive dissonance of potential nonvirgins who attitudinally are permissive but behaviourally are not. Based on the literature, we hypothesized that certain variables might explain the permissive attitudes of the potential nonvirgins while other variables would explain their nonpermissive behaviour. We found that non-virgins in comparison with potential nonvirgins were more likely to be involved in a serious dating relationship and had more friends who were sexually experienced. However there was no difference in religiosity between these two groups. On the other hand, the adamant virgins were considerably more religious than the potential nonvirgins and had fewer sexually experienced friends.

In the transitional state from virginity to nonvirginity a teenage girl is clarifying her attitudes regarding premarital sex and is beginning to view intercourse as a desirable, pleasurable activity. In this transitional state, the peer group is important not only in providing attitudinal support for sexual involvement but even more importantly by providing experienced role models. Through learning about the actual sexual experiences of her friends the teenage girl can more readily anticipate what being sexually active means. Young women today are more likely to discuss their sexual feelings with other women and finding out that other women have sexual urges provides them with group support for their own sexual feelings. Those who are sexually active serve as a role model for their non-sexually active friends. Not uncommonly, an adolescent may change her attitudes toward virginity because she knows some of her friends have enjoyed sexual relations and they have not apparently suffered serious consequences. A university female commented:

A major factor that encouraged me to engage in premarital sex was the university environment. My first year I found out that many girls were sleeping with their boy friends.

Religiosity was strongly related to sexual permissiveness with the more religious women being less accepting of premarital intercourse. The more religious are not only conforming to the more traditional religious dictates regarding premarital sex but are also more likely to follow conservative parental norms.

Low religiosity combined with high peer group permissiveness may set the stage for transition-proneness and anticipatory socialization. This is shown in the reasons given for not having intercourse with the potential nonvirgins stating that they have not experienced intercourse because they have either not met the right person or because they do not feel ready for this. Although the potential nonvirgins are accepting of premarital intercourse, they are not in an acceptable situation which would permit them to put their permissive attitudes into practice. Not surprisingly then, the dating commitment variable is crucial in distinguishing the potential nonvirgins from the nonvirgins. Whereas most of the potential nonvirgins are not involved in a committed dating relationship, most of the nonvirgins are.

Our findings suggest two stages in the progression from virginity to nonvirginity. In the first stage sexually permissive attitudes are facilitated by low religiosity and high peer group permissiveness. In the second stage these attitudes are put into practice when the girl becomes involved in a committed love relationship. The first stage of transition-proneness is, of course, dependent upon permissive peer group attitudes. In the 1950's and early 1960's when adolescents were less accepting of premarital sex, this stage of transition-proneness was generally missed. When young women engaged in premarital sex because they were in a love relationship, they lacked peer group support and thus many felt guilty. Because of the greater acceptability of premarital intercourse among many young people today, the peer group is likely to be far more supportive than it was during the 1960's.

In conclusion, as long as sex researchers continue to compare virgins and nonvirgins without regard for the possibility that some of the nonvirgins might be accepting of premarital sex, we can anticipate that sexual attitudes will only be moderately predictive of sexual behaviour. By analyzing virginity subgroups, we can better understand some of the important dynamics involved in the transition from virginity to nonvirginity.

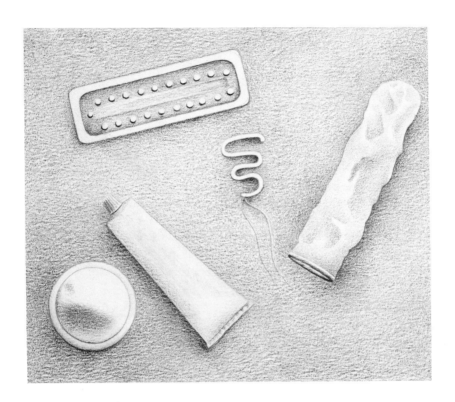

Contraceptive Methods for Young People

In this chapter the different methods of contraception which are relevant for young people will be presented. For each method the advantages and disadvantages will be discussed as well as problems and considerations involved in using that method. Because only methods relevant for adolescents will be discussed, the topic of sterilization will be omitted. Rather than going into great detail about each method, I have tried to emphasize the most relevant features. A common error of birth control educators and counsellors is to provide so much detail about each method that the adolescent is overwhelmed with facts much of which he or she does not need to be able to use contraception properly.

In comparing the different contraceptive methods we need to be aware of the fact that while there are some similarities between the contraceptive needs of adolescents and adults, adolescents have a number of additional problems or concerns. These include:

— for many adolescent females menstrual cycles are not yet regular enough to determine the time of ovulation accurately
— most adolescents do not want to become pregnant and would view an unwanted pregnancy as highly traumatic
— intercourse usually occurs on a sporadic basis and is often unplanned
— many adolescents have a romantic view of sexuality and birth control and feel guilty about planning ahead
— many adolescents are embarrassed about obtaining and using birth control
— confidentiality is a major concern and most do not want others, especially their parents, to know they are using birth control.

Effectiveness

The first question people ask about a contraceptive method is "How effective is it?" Effectiveness can be categorized as either theoretical effectiveness or use effectiveness. The theoretical effectiveness of a contraceptive method is obtained by examining its success rate when that method is used perfectly according to instructions. Of course many people do not follow instructions perfectly. Therefore, the use effectiveness category takes into account both those who use a method perfectly and those who are not as careful.

One method of analyzing effectiveness rates is by the life table method which answers the question: "Of 100 women who start and continue to use a method, how many will become pregnant in the first year?" (Hatcher et al., 1982.) Because effectiveness rates are highly influenced by the types of people using a particular method, different studies have recorded different effectiveness rates. Hatcher et al. (1982) have attempted to synthesize effectiveness rates obtained from different studies and the rates given in this section will be based upon their analysis. Rather than using the categories of theoretical and actual failure rates, Hatcher et al. (1982) are now using the categories of lowest observed failure rate and failure rate in typical users. We need to be extremely cautious in interpreting effectiveness rates because they are so dependent upon the motivation and commitment of the contraceptive user. Individuals who are poorly motivated may experience contraceptive failure with even the most effective methods while the highly motivated individual may be quite successful in using methods which are considered to be moderately or poorly effective.

Oral Contraceptives

The pill is by far the most popular method of birth control among young people. Indeed many young people equate the pill with birth control. Despite possible health hazards, adolescents strongly prefer the pill because of its proven effectiveness and because of the spontaneity in sexual relations it allows.

The two basic types of oral contraceptives are the combination pill consisting of estrogen and progestin (synthetic progesterone) and the progestin only pill. Other pill variations are the biphasic and the triphasic. The biphasic pill maintains a constant dosage of estrogen throughout the menstrual cycle along with an increase of progestin in the second half of the cycle. The triphasic pill more closely mimics the normal hormonal changes occurring during the menstrual cycle by providing low levels of estrogen in the early and late parts of the cycle with a peak at mid-cycle. The progestin level gradually rises from low levels in the first part of the cycle to higher levels in the latter part of the cycle. Both estrogen and progestin act to suppress ovulation. Progestin also makes implantation difficult by inhibiting the lining of the uterus and thickening the cervical mucous so that sperm cannot pass through.

Effectiveness

The lowest observed failure rate for the combined oral contraceptive pill is almost zero percent while for the progestin only pill it is one percent. The typical user failure rates are two percent (Hatcher et al., 1982). The most significant factor in pill failures is having to remember to take the pill consistently. Women who are forgetful and find it difficult to remember to take the pill on a daily basis would be well-advised to consider other means of contraception. If we were to consider those women who discontinue use of the pill but do not begin using another contraceptive method, then the user effectiveness failure rate for the pill might be considerably higher. Often young women who are on the pill will discontinue its use if they break off their relationship with their boyfriend. Subsequently, they do not anticipate future sexual relations and are not contraceptively protected when they begin a new relationship. One of the psychological pitfalls of pill use is that the feeling of being contraceptively protected becomes so taken for granted that when the pill is discontinued some women still continue to believe that they cannot become pregnant.

Use

Most of the combination pills are taken for three weeks beginning on day 5 of the menstrual cycle. Then for one week no pills are taken to permit menstruation to occur. The progestin only pill is taken on the first day of menstrual bleeding and taken each day even when menstruation occurs. For more specific detail see Hatcher et al. (1982).

Not all women can use the pill. There are a number of *absolute contra-indications* to pill use which are listed below. Most of these are rarely found among teenagers:

(1) a malignant tumour of the breast or reproductive system
(2) a past episode of thrombophlebitis (inflamed veins) or pulmonary embolism (lung clot)
(3) heart attack, or evidence of heart or blood vessel disease involving the brain
(4) liver malfunction
(5) hypertension (high blood pressure)
(6) undiagnosed or abnormal genital bleeding
(7) known or suspected pregnancy.

Advantages

— Because of its high reliability, the fear of pregnancy is removed for women taking the pill. This psychological freedom from the fear of unwanted pregnancy is for many young women the greatest attribute of the pill.
— For many couples the pill provides the opportunity for greater sexual pleasure because sexual behaviour can occur on a spontaneous basis without interruption to insert a contraceptive device. Also, the female may be willing to participate in sex more frequently because she no longer is worried about pregnancy.
— Women with premenstrual tension, painful periods and heavy bleeding greatly appreciate relief from these difficulties provided by the pill. There is also less anxiety over menstruation when the menstrual cycle is regularized.
— In addition to reduced menstrual disorders, there are other health benefits of taking the pill including a decreased incidence of pelvic inflammatory disease, benign breast tumours, ovarian cyst formation and iron deficiency anemia.

Disadvantages

— The main disadvantage of the pill is its physical effects on various parts of the body. Although most are minor in nature, a few are potentially fatal. Some of the side effects are estrogen-related and others are progestin-related. Many of these side effects disappear after two or three cycles of pill use or can be eliminated by changing the dosage or brand of pill. Among the side effects considered as minor are break-through bleeding and spotting, nausea, abdominal bloating, headache, irritability, mood changes and vaginal discharge. Young women commonly report side effects such as weight gain and breast discomfort. Although some of these physical changes may be viewed as minor by health professionals, they may be magnified by adolescents who are especially conscious of their physical appearance. Even a small change in weight or the occurrence of acne may be sufficiently distressing to a teenage girl so that she decides to discontinue pill use.

— The most serious disorders are blood clots, tumors of the liver and gall bladder disease. Hatcher et al. (1982) advise that users of the pill be on the look-out for the following danger signals:

severe pain in the abdomen, chest, or leg,
severe headaches,
shortness of breath, or
eye problems.

Patients should be strongly advised to call a clinic or a physician immediately if they are experiencing any of these symptoms.

— Some birth control pills may decrease sexual response. In some of these cases adding a small amount of estrogen to the pill dosage can remedy the problem. However, in other cases the decreased sexual response may result from guilt feelings about taking the pill and sexual counselling would be required to deal with these feelings.

— A sexual disadvantage of being on the pill for some women is that they believe that it is more difficult to say no to the sexual advances of men because they are on the pill. Others may believe that their sexual desires would be harder to control if they were on the pill.

I didn't want to have sex but I was on the pill so felt I should go ahead.

To justify being on the pill I felt like I should be having sex on a regular basis.

I was afraid of taking the pill because I thought that once you take the pill you would go to bed with anybody. There is nothing to stop you and I didn't like the idea of my going to bed with everybody.

— Some women should not take the pill because they lack the discipline required to take the pill regularly.

I am a very forgetful person so that I would forget three or four times a month which meant that I might as well not be taking the pill.

Notes to Family Planning Educators and Clinicians

It is important to acknowledge the possibility of side effects but to put the risks into perspective. For example, the health risks from smoking are far greater than those from using the pill. Given that the health risks are much greater for those who take the pill and smoke, counsellors should advise young women against smoking if they are on the pill or alternatively if they cannot give up smoking to seriously consider another contraceptive method.

In discussing health risks it is important to emphasize that for young women there is a very low frequency of occurrence of the most serious health risks. Current research suggests the possibility of serious health risk to the average healthy woman from use of the pill is minimal. In comparison, the possibility of serious complications, including death, is far higher for pregnancy than for pill use (Tietze et al., 1976). Nevertheless, if a woman is highly anxious about the possibility of side effects, she might be well-advised to consider alternative methods. Women concerned about side effects are very likely to discontinue pill use.

The greatest pregnancy risk for young women occurs when they stop taking the pill. In some cases women stop taking the pill on the advice of their physician who recommends "taking a rest from the pill". Often women will discontinue pill use after reading a media "scare" story which sensationalizes a particular side effect. There has been a significant increase in the number of abortions resulting from women who stop taking the pill but do not use any other contraceptives because they think they are still protected (Badgley et al., 1977). For this reason it is important to instruct young people in other methods of birth control.

Caution needs to be exercised about suggesting women go off the pill every few years in order to give their body a rest. There are many experts who disagree that this is necessary and they point to the increased chance of pregnancy resulting from such rest periods.

Although most young women who engage in regular sexual activity prefer using the pill, this is less true for those who have sex infrequently. The latter group may be well-advised to consider other methods of contraception. Those who engage in intercourse only once or twice a month usually have a more difficult time maintaining the commitment of taking the pill on a daily basis.

Finally, if it were not for the use of the birth control pill among so many young people, the numbers of unwanted pregnancies among this age group would be substantially larger. Thus we need to balance concern for side effects with the high reliability of the pill and the fact most young people believe this method is the best for their sexual relationship. In a study of university students in Ottawa, the pill was ranked far ahead of the other methods as the most satisfactory one to use. Even though one-half of the women reported experiencing some side effects from the pill, satisfaction with the method was very high (Pool and Pool, 1978).

The following two quotes from university females illustrate the sentiment of most young women today regarding the pill:

I chose the pill because of its rate of effectiveness. Every now and then I worry about the safety of it and its effect on my body yet I continue to rely on this method.

I like the pill because it's the most effective method and the easiest to use. You don't have to worry about saying "wait a minute, dear" and rushing off to the washroom.

Spermicides

Spermicides contain a chemical which kills sperm rapidly on contact. The main types of spermicides are foam, cream or jelly. Another type of spermicide is a suppository such as Encare Oval.

Effectiveness

The lowest observed rate of foam is 3-5% while the typical user failure rate is given by Hatcher et al. (1982) as 15%. There are several reasons for the relatively high failure rate of foam:

— not inserting the foam high enough into the vagina,
— using too little,
— failing to shake the foam container vigorously enough,
— failing to recognize the foam bottle is empty,
— not having the bottle available,
— not using it because of being carried away by the passion of the moment,
— douching too soon after intercourse.

(Hatcher et al., 1982, p. 92)

The major problem is having intercourse without using foam each time.

Advantages

— A prescription is not required.
— The spermicides can provide additional lubrication.
— Some protection is provided against transmission of sexually transmitted diseases.

Disadvantages

— Many couples do not like using spermicides because they believe these methods are too messy and too much bother to use. Insertion also interferes with the spontaneity of intercourse. Since spermicides should remain in the vagina for at least six to eight hours after intercourse, many women are bothered by the leakage from the vagina.
— Spermicides have an unpleasant taste which can interfere with oral-genital sexual relations.
— The effectiveness of the spermicide is short-lived and requires reinsertion for each act of intercourse.

Notes to Family Planning Educators and Clinicians

The perceived messiness of spermicides puts them at a disadvantage in comparison with other contraceptive methods. Because of this they are unlikely to be used by many young people. A high failure rate might be expected if the users have a strong dislike for this method. Spermicidal suppositories may become more popular with young women, because many will find its insertion to be more aesthetically pleasing than that of foam. In a clinical study of 50 women in Ottawa using Encare Oval over a one year period, Dr. B.N. Barwin (1982) reported that there were no pregnancies and only two drop-outs because of the side effect of a burning sensation in the vagina. However, until further research is done, we need to be cautious about effectiveness rates.

Intrauterine Device

The intrauterine device (IUD) is a foreign body which is placed in the woman's uterus by a physician. The most common types are Lippes Loop, Saf-T-Coil, Copper 7, Copper T, and Progestasert. The specific contraceptive action of the IUD is not definitely known. Most likely it interferes with the egg's ability to implant itself in the uterine wall.

There is considerable ignorance among young people about the IUD. In the study of university students in Ottawa, Pool and Pool

(1978) found that few knew the IUD was inserted in the uterus and that a physician was required to insert it.

Effectiveness

The lowest observed rate for the IUD is 1.5% and the typical user failure rate is 4% (Hatcher et al., 1982). The differing types of IUDs have different effectiveness rates. Other factors affecting use effectiveness are the experience of the clinician inserting the IUD, and the likelihood of expulsion by the patient.

Use

Many physicians prefer to insert the IUD at the time of menstruation. Women should check their IUD strings every few days for the first couple of months. After that strings should be checked at least once a month right after the period and any time when bleeding or abdominal pain occurs. To provide additional contraceptive protection women should use a barrier method of contraception for the first month after the IUD has been inserted.

Women using the IUD should be familiar with the basic warning signs of possible infection or pregnancy:

— pelvic pain or painful intercourse
— unusual bleeding or discharge
— missed period
— fever
— missing string

If any of these conditions occur, the woman should call her physician or a birth control clinic at once.

Certain IUDs require replacement at regular intervals. Progestasert users require replacements at one-year intervals and users of Copper 7 or Copper T require replacements at two-year intervals.

Advantages

— The major advantage of the IUD is that once it is inserted no further contraceptive motivation is required except for the first month of use. For couples with low motivational levels who are careless in their use of barrier methods the IUD is particularly advantageous. It is also useful for mentally handicapped women who might find other methods complicated to use.
— Many couples appreciate the spontaneity in sexual activity which is permitted by the IUD.

Disadvantages

— Bleeding is often heavier for women with IUDs.
— Menstrual cramps may become more severe and there may be spotting between cycles. These are the most common reasons for removal of the IUD.
— Some women spontaneously expel their IUDs from the uterus leaving them vulnerable to pregnancy.
— If pregnancy occurs with the IUD in place, there can be serious health risks. These health risks may be potentially fatal if an infection also occurs. Of those pregnancies that do occur with an IUD in place, some are carried to term, some are spontaneously aborted and some are ectopic.
— Although rare, perforation of the uterus, occurring mainly at the time of insertion, is a risk.
— Pelvic infection which may permanently impair future fertility is more likely to occur with the IUD than with other contraceptive methods.
— The IUD can have an adverse effect on sexual relations. The increased bleeding might inhibit intercourse during the menstrual period and longer periods may mean fewer days available for intercourse during each cycle.

Notes to Family Planning Educators and Clinicians

As with other contraceptive methods, the motivation of the patient to use the IUD is of particular importance. Patients who are highly motivated to use the IUD can better tolerate discomforts associated with it than can the less motivated. In educating young people, the possibility for pelvic inflammatory disease should be discussed.

Most importantly, potential users of the IUD should be informed that a skilled clinician can greatly reduce the probability of serious side effects. There is a strong relationship between complications arising from an IUD and the skill of the physician who inserts it. Unfortunately family planning educators sometimes present the image that all physicians have equal ability in inserting the IUD. Because the complications of the IUD are potentially serious, patients should be informed about which physicians are the most experienced with IUD insertion and who have patients with the lowest complication rates.

Family planning professionals need to evaluate the advantages and disadvantages of providing young patients with IUDs. Some clinicians are so concerned about the possibility of serious health risks that they no longer provide IUDs for teenagers.

Condom

The condom is a sheath of rubber or plastic (sometimes animal membranes) which is worn on the erect penis during intercourse. It acts as a barrier to prevent the transfer of sperm from the penis to the vagina.

Effectiveness

The lowest observed failure rate for the condom is 2 pregnancies per 100 woman years while the typical user failure rate is 10%. Used with spermicides the effectiveness rate is close to 100%, (Hatcher et al., 1982). Among university students in Ottawa, Pool and Pool (1978) found that about one-third of those using condoms on a regular basis had not used it every time intercourse occurred.

Use

The condom must be used every time intercourse occurs. It should be unrolled all the way to the bottom of the erect penis before vaginal penetration occurs. If the condom does not have a nipple tip some space should be left at the end of the condom for the semen to collect. If a space is not left the increased pressure of the ejaculate could cause the condom to break. The condom should be withdrawn as soon as possible after ejaculation to prevent it from slipping off the penis. During withdrawal of the penis the rim of the condom should be firmly held to prevent semen from leaking out. If additional lubrication is desired, spermicides or saliva or K-Y jelly could be used. Vaseline should not be used as it could cause condom deterioration. Condoms should not be re-used.

Advantages

— Within recent years there has been an increase in condom use primarily because it is free of side effects. It is particularly likely to be used in situations where intercourse is infrequent and has not been regularized sufficiently for the female to feel that she is ready to use the pill.
— Condoms are available without a prescription and thus do not require a medical examination.
— Condoms are particularly useful when couples believe that contraception is primarily the male's responsibility.
— For males having a problem with premature ejaculation, condoms can help to slow down sexual excitement and delay orgasm.

— Condoms can be effective in providing protection against sexually transmitted diseases. This is especially important for those having multiple sexual partners.

Disadvantages

— Many young couples do not use the condom because they believe it interferes with their sexual enjoyment by interrupting the sexual experience and/or diminishing the physical sensation. Some males have difficulty maintaining an erection with a condom and because of decreased sensation may be unable to ejaculate. Young women may believe that the condom is "not natural" and worry that their partner's pleasure may be diminished.
— The condom requires anticipation of intercourse and many adolescents believe that it is unromantic to plan ahead for intercourse.
— Although condoms do not require a prescription, young people are often embarrassed about purchasing condoms in a pharmacy. Young women are more embarrassed about purchasing condoms than any other contraceptive device.
— An emotional factor deterring condom use is the negative image some people have of condoms. Condoms are sometimes associated with promiscuity, prostitution and sexually transmitted diseases. By promoting the use of condoms as a means of preventing sexually transmitted diseases, we may unintentionally be reinforcing the negative image of condoms. Most young people are not as concerned about preventing sexually transmitted diseases as they are about preventing pregnancy.
— Condoms require male cooperation and some males simply refuse to use them. In a study of abortion patients, Badgley et al. (1977) found that the most common reason for stopping the use of condoms was that the partner objected to using them.

Notes to Family Planning Educators and Clinicians

The effectiveness of condoms has been misperceived by many educators and subsequently by many young people. If the condom is used correctly and used every time, its effectiveness rate is very high. Used in conjunction with foam the effectiveness rate is as high as that of the pill.

Two researchers, Dr. M.J. Free and Dr. N.J. Alexander, have suggested that if the purpose is contraception then the condom need not be placed on the penis before penetration of the vagina, only before ejaculation. In analyzing samples of pre-ejaculatory fluid from ten volunteers they concluded that the possibility is slight that pre-ejaculate sperm will be present in sufficient numbers to cause conception. (Public Health Reports, Sept. 1976, p. 442). However, further research is needed to settle this question and in the meantime caution about this is recommended.

In preventing sexually transmitted diseases it is essential that the condom be in place prior to intercourse. Also given the fact that sexually transmitted diseases can be spread from oral-genital contact, it is recommended that in casual sexual experiences the male wear a condom during oral-genital sex.

One means of reducing contraceptive embarrassment would be to have contraceptives more readily available as they are in many other countries. Few countries of the world require that condoms only be sold in pharmacies. As many personal hygiene products are sold in department stores and supermarkets, there is no reason why condoms could not also be sold in these types of outlets. Also as a means of reducing embarrassment, contraceptive advertising should become more commonplace, particularly on television.

Some family planning educators recommend that condoms not be stored in places where they are subject to heat deterioration such as in wallets or the glove compartment of cars. However, with condoms manufactured from plastic this is not a problem. By discouraging males from storing condoms either in a wallet or in their glove compartment of their car, we may actually be unintentionally discouraging males from using condoms because those are two of the most likely places in which condoms might be stored.

Diaphragm

The diaphragm is a dome-shaped rubber cup which is flexible and can be bent in half to be placed into the vagina. Once inserted it springs back to its original shape. The diaphragm fits against the cervix to prevent sperm from entering the uterus and should be used with a spermicide.

Effectiveness

The lowest observed failure rate is 2% whereas the typical user failure rate is 10%, (Hatcher et al., 1982). In one study a high success rate was attributed to a thorough educational program and careful fitting (Lane, 1976). Also the personnel believed in the method and had the skill and patience to teach it thoroughly. The detailed instruction helped to assure correct use but even more importantly bolstered the self-confidence of the person using the method so that she was more likely to use it effectively. The patient was required to demonstrate immediately following fitting that she was able to place the diaphragm properly and to remove it. She was also asked to return after one week in order to check the fit of the diaphragm and her technique of insertion.

Use

It is essential that the diaphragm be well-fitting or else it may cause physical problems resulting in disuse. The jelly or cream should be placed in the diaphragm before insertion. The diaphragm can be inserted in the vagina up to six hours before intercourse. After intercourse it must be left in place for at least six hours without douching in case there are still live sperm in the vagina which may be able to reach the uterus. If intercourse occurs more than once within the six-hour period, additional spermicidal cream should be applied on the outside of the diaphragm without dislodging it.

Advantages

— Correctly fitted and used consistently with spermicide, the diaphragm is a highly effective method not involving systemic side effects.
— The diaphragm used in conjunction with spermicide provides some protection against sexually transmitted infections.
— If used during menstruation, the diaphragm can act as a barrier preventing blood from entering the vagina during intercourse.

Disadvantages

— Because use of the diaphragm is more complicated than that of other contraceptive devices, a significant percentage of patients do not insert it correctly the first time and need to be taught how to do it again. This may prove to be frustrating and discouraging to the clinician and the patient.
— Many couples find the spermicide that accompanies the diaphragm to be messy.
— When sex is not planned ahead of time couples have to break off lovemaking to insert the diaphragm. This may discourage use particularly during the height of passion.
— Some women are uncomfortable with touching their own genitals and thus may not feel comfortable using the diaphragm. This is especially true for women with less education. Badgley et al. (1977) found that diaphragms were less likely to be used by women with low education.

Notes to Family Planning Educators and Clinicians

For diaphragm use to be successful, careful and detailed instruction regarding its use is essential. This requires patience, tact and understanding on the part of family planning counsellors. An impatient or unsympathetic attitude on the part of the professional will easily discourage diaphragm use. Some clinicians routinely discourage patients from using the diaphragm because of frustration over the difficulty patients have shown in learning how to use this method.

It is essential to tell patients the diaphragm *must* be used every time intercourse occurs. Hatcher et al. (1982) suggest that one cause of pregnancy among diaphragm users occurs among those trying to combine use of the diaphragm with a "casual" attempt at using the rhythm method. Unfortunately many in this group try to guess their fertile times rather than maintaining reliable records of their cycle.

Cervical Cap

The cervical cap is a cup-shaped object which fits over the cervix. It is held in place over the cervix by suction. Hatcher et al. (1982) recommend a cervical cap for a woman who would like to use a diaphragm but is unable to because of physical problems with it. An advantage of the cervical cap is that it can be maintained in place much longer than a diaphragm. The lowest observed failure rate has been 2% and the typical user failure rate has been 13%. Further research is needed to determine the effectiveness of this method.

Contraceptive Sponge

The contraceptive sponge has been granted approval by the U.S. Food and Drug Administration. It is expected to be granted approval by Health and Welfare Canada sometime in 1984. The contraceptive sponge is a barrier device made of polyurethane. Although similar in functioning to the diaphragm, it is simpler to use in that one size fits all women and it will be available at pharmacies without the need for a prescription. Because it already contains a spermicide (nonoxynol-9) there is no need to apply additional spermicide as is the case with the diaphragm. The sponge absorbs the ejaculate and traps the sperm so they cannot enter the cervix while the spermicide inactivates the sperm. In the United States, sponges have been approved for use over a 24 hour period, during which time they can be used repeatedly. Its effectiveness appears to be as high as a diaphragm used with a contraceptive cream or jelly (Hatcher et al., 1982).

Withdrawal

The withdrawal method requires the male to withdraw his penis from the vagina prior to ejaculation. Use of withdrawal is common among younger teenagers having intercourse for the first time.

Effectiveness

The lowest observed failure rate is 16% and the typical user failure rate is 23% (Hatcher et al., 1982). The main reason for the failure rate is that it requires a considerable amount of self-control on the part of the male and requires him to withdraw at the most pleasurable moment. For young males experiencing intercourse for the first time ejaculation tends to occur relatively quickly because of their heightened arousal and their anxiety. When using withdrawal it is absolutely essential that ejaculation take place away from the entrance to the vagina so as to prevent sperm from entering the vagina. It is also speculated that sperm may be present in the pre-ejaculate, particularly if intercourse is following recent ejaculation.

Advantages

— The advantage of the method is that it does not require a visit to a physician or purchase of a device.
— It does not require planning ahead of time.
— Withdrawal is useful in those situations where a contraceptive device is not readily available.

Disadvantages

— This method can leave the male and female feeling sexually frustrated unless other sexual techniques are introduced to bring on orgasm.
— Both the male and female may be anxious about whether or not the male will withdraw in time.
— The method is messy.

Notes to Family Planning Educators and Clinicians

While withdrawal as a method of birth control is less effective than other methods, it provides better protection than using no method at all. Educators need to be cautious about being so negative about withdrawal that young people will decide that they may as well risk complete intercourse rather than using withdrawal which provides at least some protection. In some countries withdrawal is the main method of contraception and is practised with relatively high effectiveness.

Natural Family Planning

Natural family planning attempts to prevent conception by periodic abstinence from intercourse during the fertile period of the woman's cycle. Previously this was based on the calendar method. Today the most common techniques for determining the fertile period are the sympto-thermal method and the mucous or Billings method.

The sympto-thermal method is based on the fact that the basal body temperature is lower prior to ovulation and rises after ovulation. If during each cycle, intercourse is avoided from the beginning of menstruation until after the basal temperature has been at a higher level for three consecutive days, conception is unlikely to occur.

With the mucous method, changes occurring in the cervical mucous help to pinpoint ovulation. Prior to ovulation the discharge from the cervix increases in volume, becomes clear and is highly lubricative. When that mucous is at its peak ovulation usually occurs within 24 hours.

Computerized devices are now available which can help to increase the reliability of natural family planning methods. These devices can be used to record the body temperature and the daily information is stored in the computer memory.

Effectiveness

The lowest observed failure rate of the sympto-thermal and mucous methods is 2% while the typical user failure rate is about 20% (Hatcher et al., 1982). Most failures are attributed to intercourse occurring during the pre-ovulatory period.

Advantages

— Doesn't require obtaining contraception from a physician or a pharmacist.
— Doesn't interfere with sexual pleasure when intercourse occurs.
— Sometimes young women interpret the changes in their cervical mucous as a sign that there is something physically wrong with them. Teaching them fertility awareness would decrease the anxiety associated with these misconceptions. Adolescents appreciate being more knowledgeable and comfortable about their bodies.

Disadvantages

— Complicated to learn.
— Adolescents often have irregular cycles making charting difficult.

— Couples may have difficulty abstaining during the fertile time.

Notes to Family Planning Educators and Clinicians

Many adolescents have misperceptions of their fertile period. In a study of university students in Ottawa, Pool and Pool (1978) found that relatively few could define when a woman's fertile period was. Similarly, only a third of high school students in Calgary knew the most fertile period in the female (Meikle et al., 1980). Nevertheless, some young people do make an attempt to use natural methods. It is therefore important to inform adolescents of the phases in the menstrual cycle. However, given the fact that many adolescents have irregular menstrual cycles, they should be discouraged from relying on natural family planning.

Post-Coital Contraception

Some post-coital contraceptive agents such as Diethylstilbesterol and the oral contraceptive Ovral are being successfully used as a morning-after pill to prevent pregnancy if unprotected intercourse has occurred at mid-cycle. Two tablets of Ovral must be taken within 72 hours after intercourse and again 12 hours later. Although young people should be informed of the availability of this medication, they should be strongly discouraged from relying on this as a primary means of birth control. There is still controversy over the safety of this method and some doctors will not prescribe it.

Another method of post-coital contraception is the insertion of a Copper IUD within five days of unprotected intercourse. The IUD prevents implantation of the fertilized ovum.

Although these methods have been found to be highly effective in preventing pregnancy there is the possible risk of fetal abnormality should the method fail.

Abstinence

Because family planning educators are primarily concerned with preventing unwanted pregnancies, they often ignore the educational needs of those who are not sexually active. Educators need to stress that abstinence from intercourse is a viable option and that teenagers should not feel pressured into engaging in sexual relations when they do not feel ready for it. Although about one-half of adolescents do experience intercourse by the age of 19, one-half do not and this group definitely needs the support of educators for their decision to abstain. All too often adolescents become at risk of pregnancy because they begin having intercourse before they are emotionally ready. Those who do not feel ready to engage in intercourse should be discouraged from doing so.

Young people who do not feel ready for intercourse may nevertheless have the desire to engage in sexual relations. There are many sexual techniques other than intercourse which young people can find satisfying. These can be highly pleasurable and most importantly remove the worry about a possible pregnancy.

Future Methods

Research is continuing into a diversity of alternative methods of contraception. Some methods have already been tested and found to be highly effective. These include injectable contraceptives such as Depo-Provera and skin implants both of which contain long-lasting progestins (Liskin, 1983). The advantage of these methods is that they do not interfere with the spontaneity of intercourse and do not require the daily activity of pill taking. They do disrupt the menstrual cycle so that there may be a lack of menstrual periods. Despite the fact that these methods are being used in several countries, regulatory agencies in Canada and the United States have until now not permitted these methods until the possible risk of serious side effects is clarified.

Other methods currently being tested include:

— Biodegradable implants which do not need to be removed.
— Hormone releasing vaginal rings which are inserted into the vagina around the cervix and may be left in place for up to three months.
— Reversible male methods of stopping sperm production such as gossypol, a derivative of cottonseed oil and luteinizing hormone-releasing hormone (LHRH).
— An antipregnancy vaccine.

Understanding Contraceptive Use and Non-Use

Contraceptive Attitudes and Behaviour

Most sexually active young people wish to avoid pregnancy and be responsible about contraception. Of the sexually active high school and university students in my research, 86% of the females and 81% of the males have worried that a pregnancy might have occurred.

Ninety-six percent of the young women and 92% of the young men in the student study were convinced they or their partner should use contraception if they were to have premarital intercourse. There was slightly less support for the idea of planning ahead of time to use birth control as 84% of males and 76% of females agreed they should plan ahead of time to use contraception in the event a relationship might lead to sexual intercourse.

Despite these positive attitudes to contraception, a significant proportion of young people either do not use contraception or else use less effective methods of contraception, particularly when they are first beginning to have intercourse. My research shows that only one-third of young people use any kind of contraceptive device at first intercourse. Slightly more than one-third of the high school males and females did not use any method at first intercourse compared with 25% of the university males and 22% of the university females. The methods used were mainly condom or withdrawal with about one-quarter reporting use of condom and 15% of the males and 27% of the females reporting that withdrawal was used. Few of the high school (11%) or university (18%) females were using the pill when they began to have intercourse. Similarly, among Saskatchewan youth (Weston, 1980) and also among Calgary high school students (Meikle et al., 1980) it was found that most reported using nothing or the condom at first intercourse. Meikle et al. (1980) also found that adolescent girls whose parents had a low educational level were less likely to use contraception at first intercourse.

Contraception at first intercourse is primarily a male responsibility. If he does not use either a condom or withdrawal, then chances are that no contraception will be used at first intercourse. Although these findings definitely suggest the need to provide contraceptive education for males, too often contraception is viewed as a woman's responsibility. Indeed there are many males who when having intercourse with a woman for the first time will assume she is taking the pill without even asking her.

As the sexual relationship progresses, there is generally a shift from male methods to female methods, particularly the pill. In the student study we found that during the most recent intercourse the most significant changes in contraceptive patterns were the decreased percentages not using any method (20% high school females and 10% university females) and the increased percentages using the birth control pill (35% high school and 57% university females).

For most young people contraception means either the pill, or the condom and few use either the IUD, foam, or the diaphragm. Among sexually experienced university students in Ottawa, Pool and Pool (1978) found that at some time three-fourths had used the pill and 60% had used the condom.

When asked how often contraceptive devices are used, more of the university females (68%) and males (58%) in my research than of the high school females (58%) and males (37%) said they were used all of the time. For any contraceptive method to be effective, it must be used consistently. A major reason for the greater effectiveness of the pill is that it is used more consistently than the barrier methods. For example, the pill users said that they always used a method of contraception, whereas one-half of the condom users said they always used a contraceptive device.

A Contraceptive Use Model

Although most sexually active young people attempt to use contraception it often happens that effective contraception is not used. Numerous reasons have been given for non-use of contraception and several social and psychological factors have been found to influence contraceptive use. Unfortunately no attempt has been made to integrate the diverse research studies into a theoretical model which could help us to understand more readily the processes involved in contraceptive use among sexually active young people. To integrate findings from my own research as well as from the research of others, I have developed a contraceptive use model adapted from the Health Belief Model (Becker, 1974). The main advantage of applying the Health Belief Model to adolescent contraception is the emphasis it places on motivating factors in preventive health behaviour. The major components of the contraceptive use model are: perceived susceptibility to pregnancy, perceived seriousness of pregnancy, psychological costs of contraception, cue to action, and modifying factors.

Perceived Susceptibility to Pregnancy.

Before a woman is willing to consider using birth control she must accept the possibility of becoming pregnant. With adolescents there are two aspects to consider. The first is the perceived likelihood of engaging in intercourse and the second is the realization that intercourse may lead to pregnancy. For many young people first intercourse is not seen as a planned experience but rather something that just happens. Even adolescents who anticipate that intercourse might occur do not anticipate exactly when it would occur. In my research with young people I have found the most common reason given for not using birth control is "I did not expect intercourse to occur when

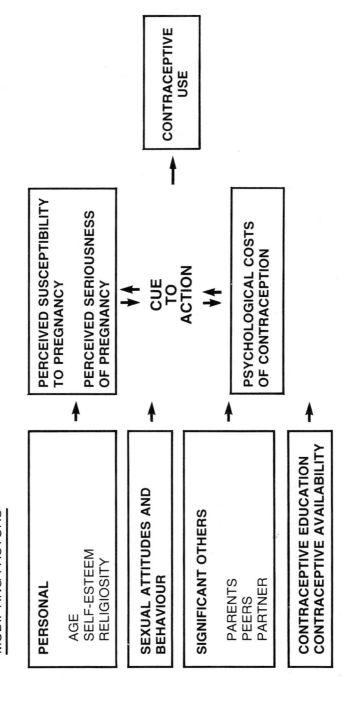

Figure 1: Contraceptive Use Model

it did." Similarly, Pool & Pool (1978) found that among female university students in Ottawa the most common reason given for not using contraception was "Didn't like to admit intercourse might occur." According to Pool & Pool this suggests a lack of preparedness to use contraception rather than a lack of motivation.

Why is first intercourse not rationally planned ahead of time? One reason is that many young people are uncertain as to whether or not they should be having intercourse. Also the decision to have intercourse is more often based on emotional factors than on rational ones and this makes rational planning more difficult especially for those just beginning to engage in intercourse. Adolescents generally assume they will not be engaging in intercourse or that at least they will not be experiencing intercourse in the near future so that they avoid the issue of contraception. Not surprisingly then, at first intercourse most young people are not contraceptively prepared.

To plan contraception one needs to perceive both that intercourse may occur and that intercourse may lead to pregnancy. Some adolescents, especially younger ones, believe they are magically protected against pregnancy. Two teenagers stated:

I never thought it could happen to me. I only thought that older people got pregnant. I just couldn't imagine myself as having a child or becoming pregnant.

I often did not see the logical consequences of intercourse namely pregnancy as a real *possibility for me. I knew that since I had reached puberty and since I was sexually active it was biologically possible for me to become pregnant. However, I felt somehow that since I was young, just having fun with my "first love", and not interested in marriage or children, I would somehow be spared.*

While some believe you cannot become pregnant until you reach a certain age, others believe you cannot become pregnant the first time you have intercourse or if you only have intercourse once in a while. Some teenagers take chances because they assume they are in their safe period of the menstrual cycle. In our study of young women at birth control clinics (Herold & Goodwin, 1980b), more of the teenagers who wanted a pregnancy test (30%) than those wanting contraception (19%) said they sometimes had not used contraception because they believed it was during their safe period. Unfortunately few adolescents have an accurate knowledge of their menstrual cycle so they may not know when their safe periods are. This is complicated by the fact that many adolescent women have irregular menstrual cycles so that it is difficult to accurately chart their safe days. Even among those who are knowledgeable about their menstrual cycle, the phenomenon of "stretching" safe days may occur. In this case the teenager who is uncertain about whether or not she is in her safe period may take a chance and assume that she is safe.

Some women who take risks by not using contraception and do not become pregnant may come to believe they are infertile. Each time they take a risk without becoming pregnant further reinforces this assumption. One pregnant teen stated:

> You know, being pregnant just doesn't seem real and even after you've had a scare. Once I thought I was pregnant and I was pretty worried but when I found out I wasn't I was back to having sex again. I figured it hasn't happened yet so I don't have to worry.

Related to the "it couldn't happen to me" perspective is the fact that some adolescents may not even think about becoming pregnant. For some thinking about the possibility of pregnancy is too anxiety-provoking. Also, at a cognitive level a teenager may understand that intercourse could lead to pregnancy while at an emotional level she may not accept this personally. In our clinic study a significantly higher proportion of those who thought they were pregnant than of those who were coming for contraception agreed with the statement "I did not really think about becoming pregnant."

One factor accounting for this apparent lack of concern about pregnancy is what Hacker (1976) refers to as sexual euphoria. In this situation the person gets carried away by his or her sexual emotions so that rational concerns such as the fear of pregnancy are blocked from consciousness. An example is when a couple has a very romantic evening combined with alcohol and high sexual desire resulting in sexual euphoria. In this situation sexual arousal can produce such an altered state of consciousness the couple may have difficulty acting in a rational manner. Consequently, people who do not ordinarily engage in risk-taking may under conditions of sexual euphoria take a chance by not using contraception. This can also happen in situations where people drink more alcohol than usual.

Saucier (1979) in a study of French-speaking adolescents living in Montreal found that one-half of the adolescents were not concerned with "here and now" prevention. Responses to questions on the adolescent's perception of vulnerability showed that many adolescents believed they would not contract any serious disease. However, age increased the perception of vulnerability and with increasing age respondents showed a greater acceptance of responsibility for their health. Saucier's findings indicate that adolescents avoid thinking about personal vulnerability for a wide range of health behaviours.

Perceived Severity of Pregnancy

A common myth about teenage pregnancy is that adolescents want to become pregnant. In fact, most young people definitely do not want to become pregnant. In my research with adolescent women I found fewer than 1% who give as a reason for not using contraception that they wanted to become pregnant. Additionally, only 1% give as a reason that they do not care whether they become pregnant. Fear of pregnancy is a very real concern among most sexually active young people and I have found that 90% have worried at some time about possibly being pregnant.

Among the minority who want to become pregnant, there is the hope that having a baby might fulfill some of their unmet emotional needs. For some having a baby is a means of getting to have someone love them. Others may view having a baby as a means of obtaining adult status and greater independence from parents. For the relatively small group of adolescents having this perspective, pregnancy is obviously viewed as a desirable experience. Consequently this group would not be motivated to use contraception. This perspective is seen more often among young women who have low educational and occupational expectations.

Experiencing a tragedy or crisis in one's life can also serve to alter one's perception of an unwanted pregnancy. Luker (1975) in her study of women having an abortion found that several had stopped use of contraception when a close family member died. Some young women may be so overwhelmed by current problems in their life that concern over the possibility of a pregnancy is pushed out of consciousness.

Another factor which may affect the perceived severity of pregnancy is the option of abortion. Given the increase in the number of abortions among women under the age of 20 in Canada, there is concern young women might be substituting abortion for contraception. In studying abortion patients in Vancouver, one physician (Hunter, 1974) concluded that because most of the women were not using contraception they were substituting abortion for contraception. Others have suggested that abortion is a back-up for failed contraception rather than a substitute for contraception (Margolis et al., 1974). In my research with students I have found that women who preferred an abortion if they became pregnant were more unlikely to use effective contraception than those who indicated they would go through with the pregnancy (Herold, 1982). Most of those with favourable attitudes toward abortion were consistently using contraceptive devices. These findings do not support the assumption that young women view abortion as a substitute means of contraception. Also, there was no significant difference in contraceptive use between subjects who had actually experienced an abortion and those who had never been pregnant, indicating that most adolescents who have had an abortion do not come to rely on abortion as a substitute means of contraception.

In another study, Evans et al. (1976) found that rather than relying on abortion as a means of preventing birth, women who had obtained an abortion were more likely to be using contraception as a consequence of having experienced the abortion.

Physicians seldom ask women directly if they view abortion as a means of birth control and instead may imply women have this view. In my research young people rarely give as a reason for sometimes not using birth control that they consider abortion an easy alternative to contraception. Health professionals as well as the general public sometimes prefer simple explanations for complex problems and thus assume that many women prefer abortion as a means of contraception without fully analyzing the emotional complexities surrounding sexuality and contraception use.

Psychological Costs of Contraception

Adults often assume that it is easy for adolescents to use contraceptive devices. In fact, there are many psychological costs involved in the use of contraception and these costs may in the mind of an adolescent outweigh the potential risks of pregnancy.

One cost of barrier methods such as foam, condom, or diaphragm is that they are believed to reduce sexual enjoyment. In addition to their messiness, these methods interfere with spontaneity. Young people often wish to romanticize sexuality and find it difficult to disrupt the sexual experience by inserting a contraceptive device. They may also be embarrassed about applying the contraceptive device in front of the partner.

Frequently adolescents haven't accepted the idea that they are sexually involved. Planning ahead to use contraception would arouse too many guilt feelings and thus they prefer instead to be emotionally carried away by the desires of the moment. This arouses less sexual guilt and anxiety. Indeed, some young women identify contraceptive preparedness with promiscuity. These women are particularly concerned that the male partner may view a woman who is contraceptively prepared as being promiscuous and "looking for sex". Given the sex role stereotype that males should initiate sexual relations, young women may try to avoid the impression that they are thinking of sex ahead of time by not being contraceptively prepared.

Not anticipating intercourse can be problematic for a young woman who has experienced intercourse but whose relationship with the dating partner has ended. For example, if she is on the pill she is quite likely to discontinue its use because she believes there is no need for birth control protection. Consequently when she begins dating again she will not be contraceptively protected. This can be quite risky because once a woman has experienced intercourse with one partner she generally moves into a sexual relationship with a new partner at a more rapid pace than she did with the former partner. Thus, she may anticipate intercourse occurring later in the relationship than it actually does.

Embarrassment about going to a physician or pharmacist for contraception can be a significant barrier to contraceptive use for young people, many of whom think it is awkward or difficult to obtain contraception. Embarrassment is a result of the teenager's own uneasiness and guilt but also an accurate interpretation of the judgmental way some professionals might react. Often adolescents are afraid they will be refused assistance because of their age.

> *My first experience with the medical profession in an attempt to obtain the birth control pill confirmed to me society's disapproval of what I was doing. I had to lie about my age, and the doctor gave me a fatherly lecture on the moral hazards of using a reliable method of birth control—he suggested that there was a good chance that I might become promiscuous.*

Many fear the internal exam which accompanies prescription of the pill, IUD, or diaphragm. Others fear being asked embarrassing questions, or being given moral lectures by health care providers. Many teenagers fear having to reveal they are sexually active and are concerned others might reveal this information to their parents.

> *Although we used condoms on most occasions, and failing that, either withdrawal, or timing sex during my periods, I feared pregnancy and waited with trepidation every month for the first sign of my period. I was still too embarrassed to ask my friends or the doctor about a safer method of birth control even though I was in my late teens. I thought they would think of me as promiscuous.*

Adolescents are especially embarrassed about obtaining birth control devices near to the parental home. In my study of students more than twice as many were embarrassed about obtaining the pill from a pharmacy close to home or from the family physician than about obtaining it from a clinic physician or from a pharmacy distant from home (Herold, 1981). This shows the importance of anonymity when adolescents are seeing a physician about contraception or obtaining contraceptive devices at a pharmacy. Furthermore, adolescents who fear parental discovery are faced with the problem of how to hide contraceptive devices from parents.

The fear that parents will find out they are using birth control is of real concern to many young people. The most common reason given by young women in our clinic study for going to the birth control clinic rather than to the family physician was they did not want their parents to find out. Such comments as "My doctor is a family friend" or "He would not give me pills without parental consent" indicate concern that the family physician would not keep the request for birth control confidential. The second most common reason was that they could not talk freely with their family doctor. The concern over keeping information about their sexual and contraceptive activities hidden from parents is reflected by the fact that most believed their parents would disapprove of their having intercourse.

The biggest fear I had following intercourse was that I might be pregnant. There was no birth control method employed in my first intercourse as it was unplanned. Later I relied on rhythm and withdrawal even though I knew the failure rates were high for these methods. I was afraid to use other methods that involved seeing a doctor or going to a local drugstore as I did not want anyone especially my parents to find out. Both my parents condemned premarital intercourse, particularly my father had stated that no guy wants to marry a "used" girl.

Parental support can affect the young person's use of contraception. In one study of adolescents who were using the birth control pill it was found that when a parent had accompanied the adolescent to the clinic that young person was more likely to continue using the pill than females who had not been accompanied by a parent (Scher et al., 1982).

There are differences in embarrassment related to the particular contraceptive method. Young women are more comfortable about obtaining the birth control pill than they are in purchasing other contraceptive devices. They are particularly embarrassed about obtaining condoms. Young women perceive condoms as a male responsibility and worry about others viewing them as too forward or sexually aggressive if they were to purchase condoms. Some also relate condoms to promiscuity and venereal disease. One explanation for lower embarrassment in obtaining the birth control pill is that obtaining the pill does not mean that one is necessarily sexually active. For example, some women obtain the pill to regulate their menstrual cycle. Another explanation could be that most young women have experienced purchasing other types of prescription drugs so that obtaining the pill might be viewed as being similar to obtaining other types of prescription drugs. Condoms and foam, on the other hand, are clearly identified as sexual products and are perceived differently from other pharmaceutical products.

Males are less embarrassed than females about obtaining condoms but are more embarrassed about obtaining female contraceptive devices. I have found that about one-half of the males are embarrassed about obtaining contraceptives close to the parental home with one-third being embarrassed about obtaining devices distant from the parental home. Embarrassement over obtaining contraception is thus as much of a problem for males as it is for females.

In the student study (Herold, 1981) greater contraceptive embarrassment was found among those:

— who felt guilty about their sexual behaviour,
— whose parents disapproved of premarital sex,
— whose friends disapproved of premarital sex,
— who believed contraceptive devices were difficult to obtain.

Those who had greater embarrassment about contraceptives were less likely to be using effective means of contraception.

Unfortunately many service providers worsen the problem of contraceptive embarrassment as illustrated in this letter to the editor:

This kind of "joke" not funny

Please print this letter. Lots of young people are suffering with the same problem and are too embarrassed to speak up!

I am speaking about the ignorance and rudeness of the people working in drug stores and pharmacies. The other day I went to a local pharmacy to pick up some personal necessities which the doctor advised. I am talking about birth control. When I put the article on the counter to pay for it, the response I got was truly humiliating. The checkout girl burst out laughing and was holding the article in view of another woman behind the same counter.

Well, they really got their jollies out of that, meantime I stood there wondering what it was that I did wrong!

All through my life I have been taught to respect myself, and by all means "be careful." I am 19 years old and have been married for almost one year. I have one child at home and don't plan on having any more children for some time.

I thought I was using my head about all this, but these so called people, who are hired for their good qualities, took it all as a big joke. Now if they laugh at me, being married and all, you can understand the embarrassment these single girls are experiencing. No wonder they refuse to take precautions half the time, and end up with unwanted children!

I hope these rude people (almost always women) realize that most of the time they are scaring away the young people before they even approach the counter. We are trying to take the step that everyone is telling us, but with the looks of sheer dirt shot upon us, how can anyone in their right mind think that they are doing the right thing!

Please understand, I am speaking for a great number of respectable young women. If those drug store women would just stop and think of how much harm they are doing by not being warm and understanding. If for any reason they find this letter dirty or ridiculous, they should not be working at that sort of job.

After all, who wants to be centred out and embarrassed for something they think is right.

We are only human, you know, just like you! "VERY UPSET" (Port Colborne)

(Canadian Press Clipping Service, Dec. 15, 1978)

Sex Guilt

Guilt over premarital sex is an important factor accounting for the non-use of effective contraception among sexually active teens who have not accepted the idea that premarital sex is right for them. Many adolescent females feel guilty when they first have intercourse, and these guilt feelings inhibit the use of contraception because using contraception means real commitment to sexual activity. For example, consider this statement from a 16-year-old girl who has been having intercourse for two months without using birth control.

I thought about using birth control a lot of times but I wasn't sure whether I wanted to use it, not because of birth control itself, but I guess because I didn't really feel right about having sex.

After a few experiences with intercourse I made an appointment to see about obtaining some method of birth control. I cancelled the day before I was to go. Why? Because I was afraid of becoming promiscuous. I already felt that I was well on my way and realized that it wasn't what I wanted.

This girl has not used birth control because she is not ready to accept the idea that intercourse is right for her and using birth control means commitment to sex.

In our clinic study we found that women who felt guilty about having intercourse used less effective methods of contraception and used birth control devices less consistently (Herold & Goodwin, 1980b). Guilty women were more likely than non-guilty women to give certain reasons for not using contraception. For example, guilty women reported not using birth control because they did not expect intercourse to happen and they did not want to appear as if they were planning to have sex. When women who feel guilty engage in intercourse, it is likely to be unplanned. Because having contraception available would heighten feelings of guilt and anxiety, these women prefer to be carried away by their emotions and have sex occur spontaneously.

Guilty adolescents were embarrassed about seeing a physician, having an internal examination and buying birth control at a pharmacy. They also feared parents learning about their sexual behaviour. Thus guilty females are concerned about disclosing their sexual activity to others and because of this embarrassment they delay using contraception or else they expect their partner to be responsible for providing birth control.

Using a birth control method forces the adolescent to acknowledge to herself a commitment to sexual activity. In other words, she must admit:

Yes, I have had sexual intercourse. Yes, I am going to have intercourse again. I must use a birth control method to prevent pregnancy.

Women who felt guilty said they did not know how to use birth control properly. One explanation for this is that guilty women tend to avoid contraceptive information. Exposing themselves to sex-related information would raise into consciousness the problem they are having accepting their sexuality. Because of their avoidance of contraceptive information, guilty adolescents are less likely to know how to use birth control properly or how to obtain birth control.

In summary, sexual guilt has a multi-faceted effect on inhibiting contraception and is a strong deterrent to contraceptive use. By discussing with young people the manner in which sexual guilt affects contraceptive use, we could do a much better job of educating for contraceptive responsibility.

Another cost of contraception is the fear of side effects. Adverse publicity concerning side effects for the pill or the IUD are often followed by a decline in the number of users of these methods. The Badgley Committee Report on Abortion in Canada (1977) found that many Canadian women discontinued use of oral contraceptives because of side effects which they had personally experienced or which they had heard about. In our study of clinic patients almost all (85%) knew of pill side effects. Weight gain was the most commonly known side effect with one-half having heard that oral contraceptives cause weight gain. The second most commonly known side effect was nausea with 23% reporting they had heard about this. More than 10% reported hearing of such side effects as circulatory disorders, headaches, emotional changes, menstrual problems and cancer. Side effects mentioned less frequently were fluid retention, birth abnormalities, aches and pains, skin problems, breast enlargement or tenderness, sterility, fainting, vaginal infections and hair growth. Most of these side effects were learned from the mass media or girlfriends. Given the fact that almost all young women have heard about pill side effects, a major difference between pill users and those not using the pill is that the latter are more concerned about the side effects. Women who are highly anxious about pill side effects are unlikely to begin pill use or if they do begin taking the pill are likely to discontinue it within a short period of time.

Cue to Action

A cue to action is an event or person which stimulates preventive behaviour. The intensity of the cue to action required to stimulate use of contraception varies from one person to another. For example, an adolescent girl who is highly aware that she might become pregnant and who is very concerned about the possibility of pregnancy will need less encouragement to use contraception than one who is not as concerned. Cues could be either internal, coming from within the individual, or external coming from others. An internal cue could be a delayed menstrual period. This is often perceived as a "near miss" which sensitizes young women to the possibility of pregnancy and motivates them to use contraception. Many young women come to a birth control clinic for the first time because they are worried about suspecting pregnancy.

> *I went through several pregnancy stress scares before I could finally get enough courage to see a doctor for the pill. When I finally saw a doctor it was because my period was long overdue.*

External cues could come from boyfriends, peers, or parents, mass media or a formal sex education program. Some teenage girls are highly dependent upon the male partner to provide the initiative for contraceptive use. Others believe that contraception is entirely their responsibility and do not need male encouragement. A female committed to contraception will risk male disapproval to carry out her decision to protect herself contraceptively.

Factors Influencing Contraceptive Use

Many factors influence an adolescent's decision to use contraception. These include such individual factors as age, self-esteem and religiosity. Attitudes toward sexuality and frequency of sexual activity also influence contraceptive use as does the influence of parents, friends, and one's dating partner. Finally, to be able to use contraception young people need to know how to use contraception and contraceptive devices have to be available to them.

Age

Age is an important variable influencing contraception among young people. Younger teenagers are less likely than older ones to use contraception particularly when they are beginning to have intercourse. Consequently, those having first intercourse during the early teen years have a higher risk of pregnancy than those delaying first intercourse. Despite some adolescent subfecundity, those having intercourse at 15 or younger are twice as likely to get pregnant in the first six months of sexual activity than those who wait to have intercourse until they are 18 or 19 (Zabin et al., 1979). In my student survey, of those who had first intercourse under the age of 16, 65% of the males and 40% of the females had not used any contraceptive method the first time. Comparatively fewer of those who had first intercourse when they were 18 or older, 32% of the males and 19% of the females, did not use a method the first time. In terms of medically prescribed methods, none of the females used the diaphragm or the IUD at first intercourse and none of the 13 to 15 year olds used the pill. However, 26% who were 18 or over when they first had intercourse were using the birth control pill.

In our clinic study the younger adolescents were unlikely to use effective methods of contraception such as the pill and more likely to use withdrawal or no method. Younger adolescents were also unlikely to use a contraceptive device consistently or every time they had intercourse.

Younger adolescents perceived contraceptives as being difficult to obtain and were significantly more likely than older ones to agree that:

— it is difficult for females of their age group to obtain a prescription for oral contraceptives;
— most young women do not know how to obtain oral contraceptives;
— many doctors are not willing to prescribe oral contraceptives to females of their age group.

In addition to perceiving oral contraceptives as being more difficult to obtain, younger adolescents were also more embarrassed about obtaining them. More of the younger females indicated embarrassment about having an internal physical examination, asking the family physician for a prescription for oral contraceptives, and obtaining oral contraceptives from a pharmacy close to where their parents lived.

Some explanations for the greater contraceptive risk-taking by younger adolescents were illustrated in their reasons for not using contraception. Lack of knowledge about how to obtain contraception was a significantly greater barrier to contraceptive use for younger adolescents than for older adolescents. Younger adolescents were also more likely to report they did not know how to use contraceptives properly. These findings emphasize the importance of informing young adolescents about sources of contraception and how to use contraception.

Younger adolescents were more dependent on their partner for contraception. For example, younger adolescents were significantly more likely to report they did not use contraception because they needed their boyfriend's encouragement and they also were more likely to expect their partner to provide contraception.

Self-Esteem

High self-esteem is important in overcoming sexual anxieties which may inhibit contraceptive use. Adolescents with low self-esteem find it difficult to plan ahead to use contraception because this means acknowledging to themselves the fact that they are sexually active. Since high self-esteem individuals have less need for social approval, they are less concerned about possible negative reactions to their use of contraception. On the other hand, those with low self-esteem because they fear rejection, are more responsive to the possible negative reactions of others to their use of contraception.

In the clinic study high self-esteem women:

— had more positive attitudes toward the use of birth control
— were less embarrassed about coming to the birth control clinic
— were less embarrassed about having an internal examination
— had less sexual guilt
— were using more effective contraception
— were using contraception on a more consistent basis.

Religiosity

Contraceptive use among adolescents is generally not influenced by the religious affiliation of the person, however, it is strongly related to religiosity as measured by the frequency of church attendance. To begin with, those who are highly religious are less likely to be engaging in intercourse. However, of the highly religious who are engaging in intercourse, sexual guilt often deters them from using contraception.

In the student study two-thirds of those who rarely or never attended religious services were using effective contraception, whereas only one-third of those who attended religious services once a week or more were using effective contraception.

Sexual Attitudes and Behaviour.

In both the student and clinic studies effective contraceptive users were more likely to:

— have more permissive sexual attitudes,
— have intercourse more frequently,
— have more sexual partners.

Young women with more sexually permissive attitudes were more likely to use effective contraception than those having conservative attitudes toward sex. This is because the more permissive women are more accepting of their sexual behaviour and less likely to have sexual guilt which inhibits contraceptive use.

Frequency of sexual intercourse is a key factor influencing contraceptive use. Most young women do not begin taking the birth control pill until they begin having intercourse on a regular basis. Teenagers who have sex on an infrequent basis sometimes feel less need for contraception because they may think that as they only have sex infrequently they are not likely to become pregnant. Having sex on a regular basis makes it easier to predict when sexual relations will occur and that makes it easier to plan ahead. Having frequent sexual relations is also likely to increase one's perception of the possibility of becoming pregnant.

Those who have had more sexual partners are more likely to use effective contraception. Because of their greater sexual experience they are probably more accepting of their sexuality, unlikely to have guilt feelings about sex and therefore able to plan ahead to use contraception.

Significant Others

Significant others such as parents, friends and one's dating partner are highly influential in an adolescent's decision to use contraception.

In both the student and clinic studies effective users of contraception were more likely to:

— have parents who approved of premarital sex and use of birth control
— have friends who approved of premarital sex and use of birth control

— be involved in a committed dating relationship
— have discussed use of birth control with their dating partner.

Parents, peers and one's dating partner play differing roles in influencing an adolescent to use contraception. In the clinic study I examined factors affecting a young woman's decision to use the birth control pill. In terms of knowledge about the birth control pill, two-thirds had received birth control information from their girlfriends and more than half had received information from school or reading materials. One-quarter received contraceptive information from mothers and only rarely (2%) did any receive information from fathers. In terms of specific information about the pill and how to obtain the pill, girlfriends were a far more important source of information than either parents or the dating partner. One-half had heard about side effects from girlfriends. Sixteen percent heard about side effects from their mothers and only 2% from boyfriends. Girlfriends were especially important in providing information about the birth control clinic as 87% of the teenage girls said they found out about the birth control clinic from girlfriends. Only about 1% learned about the clinic from either boyfriends or parents. Other sources of information were school, mass media and physician.

Although girlfriends were more important in providing knowledge, boyfriends were equally important in motivating the adolescent girl to use the birth control pill. Seventy-eight percent of the girls were encouraged by their boyfriend to use the pill and two-thirds were encouraged by their girlfriends. Few parents (10% of mothers and 5% of fathers) encouraged their daughter's use of the pill. There was considerable discussion with girlfriends and the dating partner about the pill as almost all of the young women had discussed this. Slightly more than half (55%) said their girlfriends had directly influenced the decision to come to the birth control clinic, and somewhat fewer (39%) were directly influenced by their boyfriends to come to the clinic.

In summary, peers provide the teenage girl with information, legitimization and support. Girlfriends are the most important source of information about the birth control pill, and teenage girls who are socially isolated in the sense of having few friends often delay getting birth control because they lack peer support. Almost all of the teenage girls planning to use the birth control pill have friends who are using the pill and two-thirds received encouragement from their girlfriends to use the pill. One stated:

In our group as soon as one girl got the fortitude to go out and get the pill because she was scared enough of getting pregnant, then the others followed her steps.

The boyfriend's influence is more in the nature of providing encouragement rather than providing information. While most of the young women were encouraged to use the pill by their partner, few acquired information from him either about the pill or about the clinic. This suggests that many males lack adequate information about birth control.

The type of dating relationship also influences the extent to which the boyfriend will provide contraceptive support. In a committed dating relationship the male is more likely to be concerned about whether or not his partner will become pregnant and therefore will either assume responsibility for using contraception himself or will encourage her to use contraception. However, in a casual relationship the male is more likely to simply assume that his partner is contraceptively protected often without even asking her. This, of course, leaves the contraceptive responsibility completely up to the woman.

Teenagers receive almost no information about birth control from their parents. Because they believe parents would disapprove of their sexual activity, few girls inform their parents of the decision to begin taking the pill (Herold & Goodwin, 1980a). Thus with the exception of the small minority of parents who have open discussions about birth control with their daughters, parents are bypassed in the decision of the teenage girl to take the birth control pill.

Furstenberg (1976) suggests that the important element in parental influence on the adolescent's decision to use birth control is not so much the imparting of specific birth control information as it is the fact that parents are providing legitimization for the young person to use birth control if she were to become sexually active. The teenager can thus find it easier to acknowledge her own sexuality and is better able to engage in rational planning in terms of birth prevention. It is the fear that parents may discover their sexual activity that prevents many adolescents, particularly younger ones, from using contraception. Because many parents cannot imagine their children as being sexually active, they find it difficult to discuss the topic of birth control.

Contraceptive Education.

Contraceptive education is obviously an important factor influencing use of contraception among young people because if they are not aware of contraceptive methods they cannot use them. Because of concern over the problem of teenage pregnancies, schools have become a major source of information about contraception for young people. This is a significant change from the 1960's when birth control was seldom mentioned in the school system. However, comparatively few schools have comprehensive programs, which include the motivational aspects of contraceptive use. In the clinic survey only one-third of the young women reported that the birth control education they received in school was adequate for their needs.

Contraceptive Availability.

Contraceptive decision-making in a community where adolescents lack easy access to birth control devices is considerably different than in a community where birth control clinics are available.

In the 1960's it was very difficult for adolescents to obtain contraceptives. Even methods not requiring a prescription such as condom and foam were difficult to obtain because they were often hidden behind the counter in pharmacies and adolescents were embarrassed about asking for them. There were few birth control clinics available for adolescents and often family physicians were reluctant to prescribe the birth control pill particularly if the women were under the age of 18. Today in most places in Canada contraceptives are generally available. For the most part pharmacists have moved away from the idea that contraceptives need to be hidden and some pharmacies even have sales on condoms. There are far more birth control clinics today and most will provide services to teenagers. Most universities have health services which will also provide contraceptive services. The main problem regarding accessiblity is for younger adolescents. Some birth control clinics and physicians will not provide contraceptive services for those under the legal age of consent. Many health professionals fear the possibility of a law suit in dealing with this age group. While legally this is a grey area, in fact, no physician in Canada has been convicted of providing contraceptive services to a minor.

In a national survey of Canadian family physicians it was found that one-third of the physicians were reluctant to provide contraceptive counselling to adolescents under 17 years of age (Badgley et al., 1977). Many physicians were uncertain whether such information could legally be given to minors and they did not want to do so without parental knowledge or consent, or in some instances, they did not want to contribute to what they considered was promiscuous sexual behaviour.

In a second national survey which included both obstetrician/gynecologists as well as family practitioners, 82% of physicians were willing to provide birth control information to minors without parental consent (Boldt et al., 1982). However, only 57% were definitely willing to provide birth control services to that age group while 29% said "perhaps" they would. Physicians in Quebec were the most willing to provide services to minors (72%) and physicians in the Atlantic provinces were the least willing (42%).

In 1983 both the Canadian Medical Association and the Canadian Bar Association recommend that young people who have reached the age of 16 should be able to get medical treatment including birth control pills or abortion without their parents' consent. In effect, these professional organizations were providing their moral support to the notion that many young people can make their own decisions about these issues.

Factors Influencing Pill Use Before First Intercourse

Most young women do not begin taking the birth control pill until they have had intercourse for some time. In the clinic study, of those who had experienced intercourse, most (59%) waited at least six months after beginning to have intercourse before coming to the clinic and 37% waited at least a year. Only 20% of those coming to the clinic for the pill had not yet engaged in sexual intercourse. Because pill users who have not yet engaged in intercourse are a select group, we wanted to compare the characteristics of this group with those who waited until after they had experienced sexual intercourse to begin using the pill.

The following characteristics distinguished pill users who had not yet experienced intercourse: (Herold & Samson, 1980).

— they were older at first intercourse
— they desired a higher level of education particularly college or university
— they had more open communication about contraception with their mothers
— they were more open in talking to their friends and dating partner about birth control before engaging in intercourse
— they were less embarrassed about going to a birth control clinic
— their mothers had higher levels of education.

Much of the research in contraception has focused on the failures of contraception and the non-users of contraception. If we are to adequately understand contraceptive motivation then we need to do more research with successful contraceptors. Young women who can rationally plan to obtain effective contraception prior to first intercourse are a minority group among teenagers. The importance of early use of contraception is underlined by the fact that teenagers who use a medical method at first intercourse are more likely to continue using effective contraception consistently than teenagers who do not use an effective method at first intercourse (Zelnik & Kantner, 1978).

Abortion

Of all the topics involved in sexuality certainly the most emotional and controversial is abortion. One needs only to read newspaper headlines to see how emotionally and politically charged the abortion issue is:

"Pro-Lifers put End to Abortions at B.C. Hospital"
"Abortion Battle's On"
"Lawyer Can't Act for 'Unborn' "

Abortion refers to the removal of the fetus from a pregnant woman's uterus at a time in pregnancy when the fetus cannot survive on its own. The crux of the abortion debate centers on whether or not the fetus is a human person with the same rights to live as any other person. On one side of this debate is the pro-life movement, which argues that the fetus is a person so that abortion is the murder of an unborn person and should be illegal. The main service provided by the pro-life movement is the offering of counselling and assistance to pregnant women to discourage them from obtaining an abortion. On the other side is the pro-choice movement which believes that the fetus is not a person until it has been born and that it should be the woman's decision to decide whether or not to have an abortion. The pro-choice group views abortion as a health issue and would like to repeal the abortion law so that women would have the same access to abortion services as they do with other medical procedures.

Most Canadians prefer not to be involved in the abortion debate and want to avoid the issue. Politicians, who by nature prefer to stay away from controversy, often wish that the abortion issue would simply go away. No matter what stand politicians take on the issue they are bound to arouse the wrath of some group whose position is opposed to theirs.

The Abortion Law

In 1969 it became legal in Canada to perform therapeutic abortions but only if a therapeutic abortion committee attached to a hospital and comprising no fewer than three doctors agrees that the continuation of the pregnancy would or would be likely to endanger the mother's life or health. The abortions have to be carried out by a qualified medical practitioner in an accredited hospital. Abortions performed outside of these conditions are considered illegal and subject to criminal prosecution.

A woman wanting an abortion first has to find a physician who will support her application. The physician will examine her and send a medical report to a hospital abortion committee, providing he or she can locate one that is accepting abortion applicants. The committee will review the physician's report and decide whether or not to grant the abortion request. If the request is accepted then space will have to be booked at a hospital for the procedure.

Most hospitals in Canada do not have an abortion committee with the result that abortions are mainly performed by a small number of hospitals in large urban areas. In certain regions of the country it is virtually impossible to obtain an abortion. In 1981 there were 267 hospitals in Canada with therapeutic abortion committees. This was a slight decline from the 274 reported for 1975 (Statistics Canada,

Catalogue 82-211, 1981). Many hospitals have quotas on the number of abortions they will perform so that the physician may have to contact several hospitals before finding one that will accept his patient. If hospitals in his community are not accepting any more abortion patients then the physician will have to refer the patient to another community and possibly to the United States.

Those opposed to the current abortion law are concerned that hospitals are not required to establish a therapeutic abortion committee. They are also concerned that many small rural hospitals lack the staff and resources to establish abortion committees and perform abortions. Other criticisms are that women applying for an abortion do not have the right to appear before the abortion committee and there is no right of appeal if the woman's application for an abortion is denied.

An important legal issue is whether or not parental consent should be required for a teenager to obtain an abortion. The situation varies across the country. For example, in Quebec, a girl may be able to obtain an abortion without her parents' consent if she is fourteen years of age or over, while in Ontario she must be 16 and in Saskatchewan she must be 18.

The most contentious issue is the definition of what might be endangering to the mother's health. While some abortion committees will accept almost any condition or situation as affecting the mother's health, including psychological and economic factors, other committees will approve abortions only in situations where continuation of the pregnancy might result in the mother's death. Liberal reformers want hospitals to adopt the broadest possible interpretation of the mother's health whereas groups opposed to abortion prefer the narrowest possible interpretation.

Groups opposed to abortion believe that no abortion services should be provided in any community; therefore, they lobby governments at all levels to prevent funding organizations involved in abortion counselling. They also lobby hospitals to prevent abortions from being performed. In some communities Right-to-Life groups have attempted to elect a majority of members to a hospital's Board of Trustees. This Board of Trustees would vote to either disband the hospital's abortion committee or else would only appoint members to that committee who were opposed to abortion.

Right-to-Life groups have also gone to court to challenge the legality of the abortion law. In 1983 former Manitoba Cabinet Minister Joe Borowski argued before a Saskatchewan Court of Queen's Bench that fetuses are protected under the Charter of Rights giving everyone the right to life, liberty and security of person. Mr. Justice W.R. Matheson disagreed and in dismissing Mr. Borowski's claim stated, "there is no existing basis in law which justifies a conclusion that fetuses are legal persons and therefore within the scope of the term everyone utilized in the Charter". (*Globe & Mail, October 14, 1983*)

The pro-choice groups, on the other hand, are lobbying to expand the provision of abortion facilities so that any woman in Canada who decided on an abortion could easily obtain one. They would like to see specialized clinics established where comprehensive medical and counselling care could be provided. They argue that the present system results in a considerable delay for women obtaining an abortion and they would therefore eliminate the requirements of having to obtain approval from a hospital committee. In the Province of Quebec, Dr. Henry Morgentaler has established private abortion clinics. For six years between 1970 and 1976 the Quebec Liberal Government had tried to convict Dr. Morgentaler of performing illegal abortions. However, three separate French-speaking juries decided that he was not committing a crime. Consequently, the Quebec government gave up trying to prosecute Dr. Morgentaler on the grounds that the law is unenforceable. In July, 1983 Dr. Morgentaler opened abortion clinics in Winnipeg and Toronto. These clinics were promptly raided by the police and Dr. Morgentaler was once again brought to trial for performing illegal abortions.

Abortion Methods

There are different methods which can be used to induce an abortion at different stages of pregnancy. The main techniques are menstrual extraction, dilation and curettage, vacuum aspiration, saline abortion and hysterotomy.

Menstrual extraction involves inserting a thin hollow plastic tube through the cervix and suction is applied to remove the uterine lining. This procedure can be performed within the first few weeks after a late menstrual period if the woman suspects she might be pregnant. In Canada the legal acceptability of this procedure is in doubt unless approved by a hospital therapeutic abortion committee. Dilation and curettage involves dilating the cervix and withdrawing the fetus by means of special forceps. The curettage is used to scrape loose all substances remaining in the uterus. The vacuum aspiration technique is similar to menstrual extraction except that the suction tube is larger and the suction force is stronger. The curettage is also used to be certain that none of the fetus or placenta remains in the uterus. Both of these procedures can be used up until the twelfth week of pregnancy and they have a low complication rate.

The saline abortion which is used after the sixteenth week of pregnancy is more complicated. It involves inserting a needle through the abdominal wall into the uterine cavity and injecting a salt solution into the amniotic fluid. Within six to forty-eight hours contraction of the uterus begins and continues until the fetus is pushed through the cervix. Another technique sometimes used to terminate a pregnancy is hysterotomy. In this procedure the fetus is removed by cutting through the abdominal wall and removing the fetus and placenta through the incision as in a Caesarian section.

In recent years abortion procedures have been simplified. In 1981, two-thirds of the abortions in Canada were performed on an out-patient basis. This is a considerable change from 1974 when only 29% of abortions were performed on an out-patient basis (Statistics Canada, Catalogue 82-211, 1981).

Most Canadian hospitals will not perform an abortion beyond twenty weeks of gestation and some will not perform the operation beyond twelve weeks. Adolescents often delay having their abortion until later in their pregnancy and this can result in a higher probability of medical complications. Younger adolescents, in particular, often deny that they are pregnant and thus put off seeking medical assistance. Also many adolescents have irregular periods so that pregnancy is more difficult to detect. Further delays are caused when adolescents do not know how to obtain an abortion or whom to contact.

Abortion Trends Among Teenagers

The number of abortions to teenage females in Canada increased from 15,082 in 1974 to 18,406 in 1981. Similarly the abortion rate or the yearly number of abortions per 1,000 women under the age of twenty increased from 13.6 in 1974 to 16.2 in 1980 (Statistics Canada Catalogue, 82-211, 1981). The number of abortions and the rate among teenagers peaked in 1979 and declined slightly in 1980 and again in 1981. Part of this decline may be attributed to an increasing number of women who choose to have their abortions performed in the United States. Because of difficulty obtaining an abortion in Canada the number of Canadian women having an abortion performed in the United States more than doubled between 1979 and 1981. Also an increasing number of women have gone to private clinics in Quebec which do not report their abortion statistics to the government.

In 1981 28.3% of all abortions were to teenage females. This was a decrease from 31.5% in 1974. Almost all (96%) abortions to teenagers were performed on single teenagers. For 81% of the teenagers, gestation at the time of abortion was 12 weeks or less (Statistics Canada Catalogue 82-211, 1981).

Among women aged 20 to 24 the number of abortions has risen consistently since 1974 and in 1981 there were 21,027 abortions in this

Figure 2: Abortion Rates Per 1,000 Females Among 15-24 Year Olds,
Canada, 1974-1981

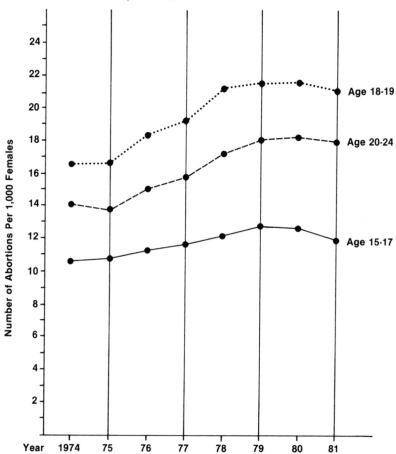

Source: Statistics Canada, *Therapeutic Abortions, 1981*,
Catalogue 82-211 (Table 59).

TABLE 4
THERAPEUTIC ABORTIONS IN CANADA 1974 AND 1981

	1974	1981
Total no. of abortions	48,136	65,053
Abortions in women under 20 years of age		
No.	15,082	18,406
% of total abortions	31.5	28.3
Abortion rate per 1,000 women under 20 years of age	13.6	16.2

Source: Statistics Canada Catalogue 82-211, Therapeutic Abortions, 1981.

TABLE 5
THERAPEUTIC ABORTIONS AMONG TEENAGE FEMALES (UNDER 20 YEARS)
BY PROVINCE, CANADA, 1981

Province	Therapeutic Abortions, females under 20 years	Abortion rate per 1,000 females under 20 years
ALL PROVINCES	18,406	16.2
Newfoundland	163	5.3
Prince Edward Island	9	1.4
Nova Scotia	566	13.5
New Brunswick	172	4.9
Quebec	1,950	6.4
Ontario	8,657	21.9
Manitoba	528	11.1
Saskatchewan	630	13.5
Alberta	2,180	20.9
British Columbia	3,452	29.5
Yukon	30	30.0
Northwest Territories	58	23.2

Source: Statistics Canada Catalogue 82-211, Therapeutic Abortions, 1981, (Tables 4, 5).

age group. Similarly, the abortion rate for women aged 20 to 24 increased from 14.1 in 1974 to 18.0 in 1981. The abortion rate has consistently been higher for women aged 20 to 24 than for teenagers. Both of these younger age groups contribute to a disproportionate share of the number of abortions. In 1981 almost two thirds of abortions (62%) in Canada were performed on women under 25 years of age (Statistics Canada Catalogue 82-211, 1981).

The number and rate of abortions varies considerably by province. In 1981 there were nine abortions performed on teenagers in Prince

Edward Island compared with 8,657 in Ontario. The abortion rate per 1,000 females under age 20 ranged from 2.0 in Prince Edward Island to 30.2 in British Columbia. The abortion rates reflect accessability to abortion as in some provinces it is almost impossible to obtain a legal abortion whereas in others it is relatively easy.

Attitudes of Young People to Abortion

In determining attitudes to abortion we need to distinguish between attitude and behavioural intention. Attitude refers to how one evaluates something whereas behavioural intention refers to the person's subjective probability of performing a behaviour. Attitudes and behavioural intentions can be inconsistent in that a woman might have a positive attitude toward abortion in general and yet not want to actually have an abortion herself. In our study of high school and university females we found that while three-quarters believed that the decision to have an abortion should be left to the woman and her physician, considerably fewer (39%) indicated they personally would want to choose an abortion. There were considerable differences between sexually experienced and inexperienced females as twice as many non-virgins (48%) as virgins (24%) indicated they would choose an abortion. Given the fact that for most of these young women having an abortion is a hypothetical situation, these percentages may be misleading when it comes to reality. For example, of those students who had actually experienced a pregnancy, 81% had an abortion.

The males were generally less approving of abortion than the females with 46% agreeing that the abortion decision should be left up to the woman and her physician. Many of the males who disagreed with this said the father should also be involved in abortion decision-making. When asked what they would prefer to do if a girl friend became pregnant only 27% said they would prefer that she obtain an abortion. However, as with the females this type of hypothetical question may underestimate what happens in reality. Of those males whose partner had ever become pregnant all of the males said the pregnancy ended in abortion.

While some people oppose abortion under any circumtances and others approve under any circumstances, many vary their approval according to the reason given for the abortion. In a survey of University of Toronto students from 1968 to 1978, Barrett (1980a) found almost all (80% or more) approving of legal abortion if the pregnancy involved risk to the woman's health, possible child deformities, or was a result of rape. About one-half approved in the situations where the pregnancies occurred out of wedlock, the child was unwanted or if the parents could not economically afford to support the child. Sexually experienced males and females were far more likely to approve of abortion under any circumstances than were the sexually inexperienced.

Among students at Carleton University and at the University of Ottawa, 37% agreed that abortion is an acceptable solution to an unwanted pregnancy; 26% disagreed; 33% said it depended on the circumstances and 3% had no opinion (Pool & Pool, 1978). More of the women thought the abortion decision should be up to the woman herself or her and her doctor rather than up to her and her partner.

Canadian Attitudes to Abortion

It is difficult to obtain accurate public opinion regarding the issue of abortion because responses vary depending upon how the survey questions are worded. For example in a Gallup Poll survey conducted in June 1982 for the Canadian Abortion Rights Action League, 72% of a random sample of adult Canadians agreed with the statement:

> *A decision on whether or not to perform an abortion should rest with the consenting patient and should be performed by a licensed physician in conformance with good medical practice.*

Twenty-three percent disagreed. Males and females were in equal agreement. Agreement was higher for those under age 30 than for those in the 50 and over age bracket. In another survey somewhat different results were obtained when the wording of the question was changed. The Gallup poll in July, 1983 asked 1,062 Canadians:

> *Do you think abortions should be legal under any circumstances, legal only under certain circumstances or illegal in all circumstances?*

The poll indicated 23 percent of those interviewed thought abortion should be legal under any circumstances, 59 percent said it should be legal only under certain circumstances and 17 percent said it should be illegal in all circumstances. One percent of respondents said they had no opinion.

Many Canadians are unaware of the abortion law and this affects their response when they are asked whether abortions are too easy or too difficult to obtain. The Badgley committee on the operation of the abortion law conducted a national survey of public opinion regarding abortion in 1976 (Badgley et al., 1977) and found that two-thirds of Canadians were not aware that it was legal to obtain a therapeutic abortion. About one-half did not know what the situation was in their community regarding the accessability of abortion services. Individuals with an elementary school education were far less informed about the abortion laws than those with a university education. In provinces where the abortion rate was higher, such as in British Columbia and Ontario, a greater percentage of people were aware that abortion was legal. Fewer than one out of ten persons surveyed said that treatment services for induced abortion were too easily accessible while one out of six said that such services were too difficult to obtain. When asked their attitudes regarding the abortion law, one-half of Canadians either didn't comment or were satisfied with the current law. One out of six women and one out of eight men felt the law was too liberal and made it too easy to obtain an induced abortion whereas a quarter of the women and a third of the men said the law was too restricted. Younger people and those with university education were more likely to view the law as too restricted. Conversely, older people and those with elementary school education thought the current law was too liberal. The Badgley committee concluded that there was no popular mandate to change the current abortion law as most Canadians supported the status quo. The committee pointed out that a person's attitude towards service accessibility depended upon whether or not that individual perceived himself or herself as needing the service. Women desiring an abortion or access to an abortion tend to view the accessibility issue in a different light than those women who believe they would never require these services.

The Abortion Decision

Abortion tends to be used as a back-up to contraception rather than as a substitute for contraception. Few teenagers consciously think ahead of using abortion as a means of contraception.

Adolescents who are unmarried are far more likely to want an abortion than those who are married. Also those who choose an abortion are more likely to:

— come from middle and upper middle class backgrounds,
— perform better in school,
— have higher educational and occupational goals (Phipps-Yonas, 1980).

Young women from lower class backgrounds are more likely to have negative feelings about abortion and also are less likely to be aware of the availability of abortion services. Better educated young women who have higher occupational goals are concerned that childbearing might interfere with educational and career opportunities. In studying a sample of pregnant Ontario teenagers Guyatt, (1978) found that those choosing an abortion said the major reason was they wanted to finish school and achieve their occupational goals. These women definitely did not want to become mothers at this point in their lives and also they believed that it would be far more traumatic to bear the child and give him up for adoption then to have an abortion.

Although pregnant teenagers may consult with others about whether or not to have an abortion most make the decision by themselves (Rosen et al., 1982). Many adolescents keep their pregnancy and abortion hidden from parents. In one study only 22% of aborters who were eighteen or nineteen years old told their parents of their pregnancy and abortion (Rosen et al., 1982). If parents were told, in the majority of cases only the mother was informed. Generally most adolescent females believe their mother can accept the pregnancy situation better than their father can. Adolescents do not tell their parents because they believe their parents would be hurt or else they don't want their parents to find out they had been sexually active. These findings reflect the difficulty many parents and teenagers have in communicating about sexual issues.

Since 1974 there has been a consistent increase in the proportion of pregnant adolescents choosing to have an abortion rather than a live birth (see Figure 3). Younger adolescents who are pregnant are more likely to choose an abortion than older ones.

Among pregnant adolescents in 1981:

— For those under age 15 there were two abortions for every live birth.
— For 15 to 17 year olds there was almost one abortion for every live birth.
— For 18 to 19 year olds there was one abortion for every four live births.

The proportion of pregnant young women who chose to have an abortion varies considerably by province (see Table 6). Among all Canadian females under 20 years of age there were 61 abortions for every 100 live births in 1981. British Columbia and Ontario had the highest proportions of teenagers choosing an abortion and in these provinces among females under 20 years of age there was about one abortion for every live birth. In Quebec, Alberta and the Yukon there was approximately one abortion for every two live births. In contrast, Prince Edward Island had one abortion for every twenty-three live births. Again, these provincial differences reflect the differential access to abortion services across the country.

Figure 3: Abortion Rates Per 100 Live Births Among Adolescents, Canada, 1974-1981.

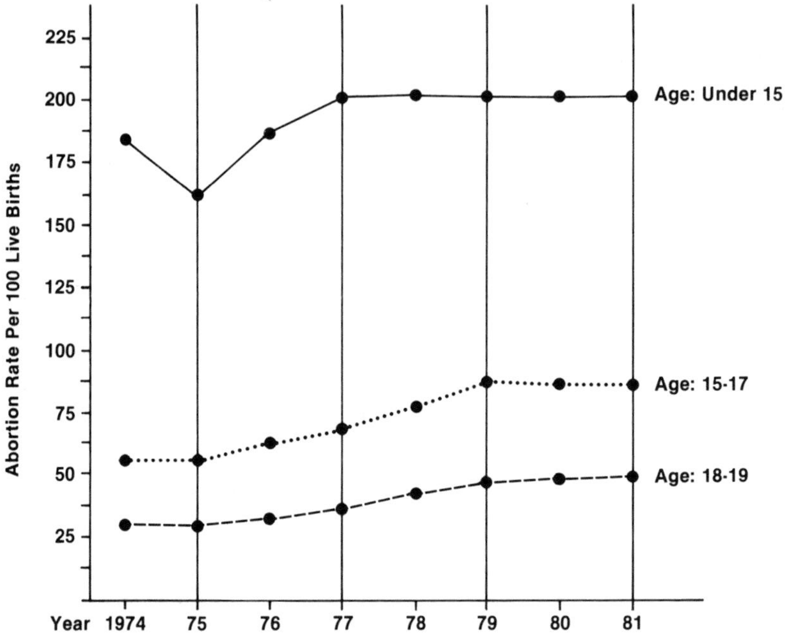

Source: **Statistics Canada,** *Therapeutic Abortions, 1981,* **Catalogue 82-211 (Table 60).**

TABLE 6
TEENAGE ABORTION RATES
PER 100 LIVE BIRTHS BY PROVINCE, 1981

Province	Rate
Canada	61.0
Newfoundland	no data
Prince Edward Island	4.3
Nova Scotia	38.2
New Brunswick	13.7
Quebec	42.6
Ontario	94.1
Manitoba	27.5
Saskatchewan	27.3
Alberta	47.5
British Columbia	101.1
Yukon	43.5
Northwest Territories	20.3

Source: Statistics Canada Catalogue 82-211 *Therapeutic Abortions, 1981,* (Table 5).

It is important to emphasize that for most women the abortion decision is not taken lightly and most find it a stressful decision to make. Among students at Carleton and Ottawa University many perceived abortion as a simple operation and yet 81% believed that abortion was likely to leave psychological scars (Pool & Pool, 1978). Regardless of the outcome, having to make a decision about an unwanted pregnancy invariably results in considerable anxiety and stress.

I can remember feeling so scared like it was the end of the world, and that there was no answer to a problem.

What are the emotional after-effects of having an abortion? The most common reaction among women after obtaining an abortion is emotional relief, a feeling that they have been relieved of a tremendous burden (Gold et al., 1979). A key factor is whether or not the woman's decision to have an abortion is supported by others. Women who are supported by close friends and/or relatives are the most satisfied, the happiest and have the least guilt. Those who are pressured into the decision are more likely to be guilty and sadder than the others (Gold et al., 1979). In a study by Greenglass (1976) only six percent of women said they were against the decision to have an abortion but were pressured into it by others. Single young women were more pressured than other women. Greenglass also reported that while some women may experience depression and/or guilt following an abortion, these feelings tend to disappear within a few months. Although most women are relieved at having the abortion many have feelings of being deviant or stigmatized. The attitudes that others have towards the abortion have a profound effect on the woman's adjustment to it.

Poorer women seem to have a more difficult time adjusting to abortion than more affluent women (Greenglass, 1976). Greenglass attributes this to the greater difficulty poor women have in obtaining an abortion as well as the fact that poor women tend to be less accepting of abortion.

The male role in the abortion process has been generally overlooked by health care professionals. This is mainly because abortion is generally viewed as a woman's issue and therefore her responsibility. Many women do not even inform their partners of the abortion especially if the sexual relationship is a casual one. Arthur Shostak, an American sociologist at Drexal University, in studying the reactions of men to abortion, reported that many need counselling to deal with their conflicted feelings about abortion. Two-thirds of males surveyed by Shostak disagreed that males involved in an abortion have an easy time of it (Sexuality Today 6, 45, 1983).

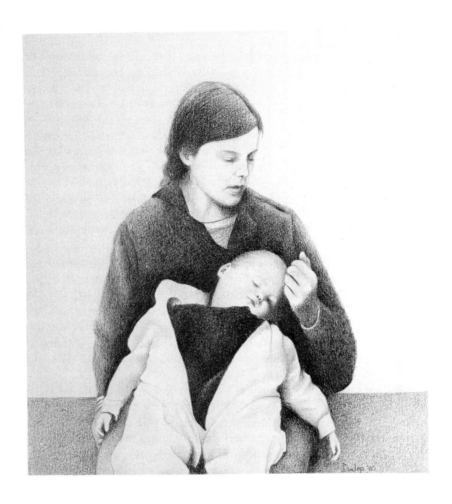

Adolescent Motherhood

Pregnancy Trends Among Canadian Youth

In examining pregnancy trends we need to be aware of the total size of the adolescent population. For the past few years the adolescent population in Canada has been declining. For example, the number of thirteen to nineteen-year-old females declined from 1.6 million to 1.5 million from 1976 to 1981 (Statistics Canada, 1981 Census). This decline has helped contribute to fewer births occurring among this age group. However, the main contributing factors have probably been the increased use of contraception and the increase in the number of abortions. Over the past twenty years there has been a large and consistent decrease in the fertility rate among adolescents. The fertility rate among 15 to 19-year-olds dropped by more than one-half from 58.2 per 1,000 females in 1961 to 26.4 in 1981 (see Figure 4).

In 1975 there were 39,188 births to teenagers of which 312 were to mothers under the age of 15. In comparison, in 1981 there were 29,330 births to teenagers of which 268 were to mothers under the age of 15. Similarly, the percentage of births to teenagers relative to the total number of births in Canada dropped from 10.9% in 1975 to 7.9% in 1981 (Statistics Canada Catalogue 84-204, 1974 and 1981).

The marital status of teenagers having live births has also changed. In 1974 live births were twice as likely to occur among married adolescents than among those who were single. However, in 1981 there were more births to single teenagers. While the number of births among married teenagers dropped significantly from 24,142 in 1974 to 11,585 in 1981, they had almost doubled among those who were single and increased from 9,870 in 1974 to 17,479 in 1981. These statistics indicate that fewer teenagers today feel compelled to get married because of pregnancy (Statistics Canada Catalogue 84-204, 1974 and 1981).

In recent years fewer teenagers have married. For example, in 1981, 17.8% of nineteen-year-olds were ever married compared with 20.3% who were married in 1971 (Statistics Canada, 1971 and 1981 Census). There are several possible explanations for the fact that fewer teenagers are getting married. One could be that more young people are planning to attend community colleges and universities and therefore are delaying marriage. Another factor is the increasing preference to live with someone before getting married. In the 1960's it was extremely rare for unmarried young couples to live together, whereas today it has become commonplace.

The most dramatic change occurring among pregnant single teenagers is the number keeping their babies. Until the late 1960's most unwed mothers gave their babies up for adoption. During the 1970's there was a sharp increase in the percentage of single mothers keeping their babies so that by 1980 approximately 80% to 90% of pregnant teenagers were keeping their babies (MacDonnell, 1981). This resulted in far fewer babies available for adoption. Some couples desperately anxious to adopt turned to surrogate mothers to produce babies for them. Another consequence has been the increase in the number of adolescent mothers receiving welfare benefits. For example, the number of single mothers in Ontario between the ages of 16 to 20 receiving family benefits doubled from 1,149 in March 1974, to 2,073 in March

Figure 4: Fertility Rate, 15-19 Year Olds, Canada, 1961-1981. (Selected Years)

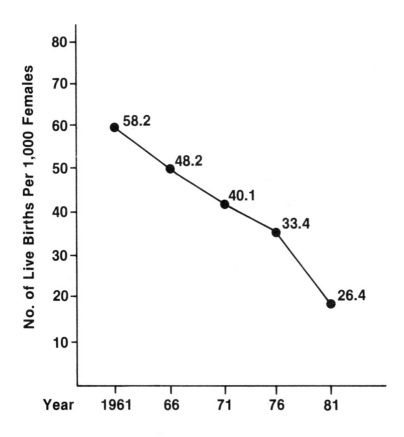

Source: Statistics Canada. *Vital Statistics: Births and Deaths,* **1981, Vol. 1, Catalogue 84-204 (Table 15).**

1980. (Ministry of Community and Social Services, Ontario Government, 1980.)

Accompanying the decline in number of adoptions has been a decline in the proportion of pregnant adolescents seeking professional counselling and assistance. In 1969 almost all new unmarried mothers in Ontario were seen by Children's Aid Societies; whereas, in 1979, only 29% were (Guyatt, 1981). Given greater societal acceptance of unwed mothers, it may be that teenage mothers today feel less of a need for professional counselling.

Who Gets Pregnant?

During the 1950's and '60's it was commonly thought that many teenagers became pregnant as a means of coping with unmet psychological needs. Current research indicates that most young people who become pregnant do so accidentally. In the Ontario study of single mothers only eight percent said they had wanted to become pregnant. In a study of 346 unmarried mothers in Nova Scotia, MacDonnell (1981) found that while most of them had not wanted to become pregnant, few had taken any precautions against pregnancy. Yet when they found out they were pregnant most immediately decided to keep the child.

Socio-economic status and educational aspirations are the strongest factors related to teenage pregnancy. Even though teen pregnancy occurs at all educational levels, those from low socio-economic backgrounds who have low educational and vocational aspirations are more likely to become pregnant (Phipps-Yonas, 1980).

Age of first intercourse also affects the probability of pregnancy, with those having first intercourse at young ages more likely to become pregnant than those who delay first intercourse. In our study of high school and university students we found that 29% of those who began having intercourse when they were under the age of 16 had experienced a pregnancy compared to only 4% of those who waited until they were 19. One obvious explanation is that those who begin having intercourse at younger ages have more opportunity to become pregnant because they have sex for a longer period of time than those who wait until they are older. Another reason is that younger teenagers are less likely to use effective means of birth control.

While the probability of becoming pregnant is greater among younger adolescents, most females wait until their later teen years before beginning to have sexual intercourse. Consequently, most teenage births occur in the older age groups. In 1981 two-thirds of all births to teenagers occurred among women aged 18 or 19 (see Table 7).

TABLE 7
LIVE BIRTHS BY AGE OF MOTHER
AMONG ADOLESCENTS, CANADA, 1981.

Age	No. of Births
11	1
12	1
13	35
14	231
15	938
16	2,749
17	5,420
18	8,472
19	11,483

Source: Statistics Canada Catalogue 84-204, Births and Deaths, 1981 (Table 4).

TABLE 8
LIVE BIRTHS TO MOTHERS 15-19 YEARS,
CANADA AND PROVINCES, 1981.

Province	No. of Births	Fertility Rate
Canada*	29,062	26.4
Prince Edward Island	211	33.5
Nova Scotia	1,472	35.2
New Brunswick	1,236	35.1
Quebec	4,540	15.0
Ontario	9,127	23.1
Manitoba	1,897	39.9
Saskatchewan	2,277	47.9
Alberta	4,567	43.6
British Columbia	3,388	29.0
Yukon	69	66.3
Northwest Territories	278	113.0

*No data for Newfoundland

Source: Statistics Canada Catalogue 84-204, Births and Deaths, 1981 (Table 4).

There are considerable variations in the teenage fertility rate across Canada (see Table 8). In 1981 the highest fertility rates among young women were in the Yukon and the North-West Territories. These may reflect the higher fertility rates of native people. Saskatchewan had the next highest rate followed by Alberta. The provinces with the lowest rates were Quebec, Ontario and British Columbia. The relatively low fertility rates in Ontario and British Columbia are to a fair extent a consequence of the higher abortion rate in these provinces. Quebec has the lowest fertility rate in Canada for teenagers and for women aged 20 to 24 years.

Keeping the Baby

Which single mothers are more likely to keep the child and which are more likely to give the child up for adoption? Research suggests that those teenagers who give up their babies are more stable and ambitious than those who keep their babies. Girls who dislike school and who have no career ambitions may believe that parenthood is the only rewarding role available to them and view parenthood as a means of obtaining adult status. Lightman and Schlesinger (1980) in a study of pregnant teenagers in Ontario maternity homes found that those planning to give their babies up for adoption were more likely than those planning to keep to have the following characteristics:

— to be in school and plan to complete school
— to be less likely to have a serious illness, handicap or to have received psychiatric treatment
— to have involved their own parents in the decision making
— to live at home with both parents.

In a study of Vancouver teenage mothers, Fallon (1978) found the most common reason given for keeping the baby was that they wanted a baby to love. Other less common reasons were to keep a boy friend, to get out of a foster or group home, to get back to their mothers or to defy the wishes of others.

Why are so many teenagers choosing to keep their babies? One explanation is that it is now easier for young mothers to obtain welfare benefits. One exception occurred in 1983 when the Province of Nova Scotia restricted financial benefits for single teenage mothers who were under the age of majority. Certainly some teenagers are more likely to keep the baby because they can rely on government funding. However, this is not the main reason. Instead the most significant factor accounting for this trend is the increased societal acceptance of unwed parenthood. Until about the mid 1960's it was considered shameful and sinful for a woman to become pregnant if she were not married. If she did become pregnant then there were strong pressures either to marry the father or else to give the baby up for adoption. In many cases the girl's pregnancy was hidden from others by sending her to a maternity home or to relatives in a distant city. Society's institutions including the church, the school and social agencies reinforced the notion that pregnancy outside of marriage was an immoral act. Consequently these institutions strongly discouraged the girl's keeping the baby. Pregnant girls, for example, were forced to drop out of school and there were no special schools for them.

During the late 1960's and early 1970's these attitudes began to change as tolerance, compassion, and permissiveness replaced condemnation. Instead of trying to persuade girls to give up their babies, social workers left it up to the girls themselves to decide.

Consequences for the Child

Several medical problems have been associated with adolescent pregnancy. In particular, the following conditions are more prevalent among adolescent mothers than among adult mothers:

— toxemia,
— anemia,
— premature labour,
— low birth weight infants,
— higher rates of infant mortality.

(*McKenry et al.*, *1979*)

The major causes of these conditions include the emotional stress of unplanned pregnancy, inadequate pre-natal care and poor diet. Pregnancy usually results in considerable emotional stress for adolescents because they are faced with the difficult problems of having to reveal to others that they are pregnant and of having to decide how to resolve the pregnancy. Because adolescents often deny their pregnancy in an attempt to hide it from others, they put off obtaining adequate pre-natal care. Furthermore, adolescent growth and pregnancy make competing demands for nutrients and the result can be detrimental both to mothers and their infants. Some pregnant teens, concerned about weight gain, may unduly restrict their diet, thereby depriving the fetus of needed nutrients.

Research (Phipps-Yonas, 1980) suggests that if adolescents aged 15 years and over receive adequate nutrition and pre-natal care then the medical risks of pregnancy are not greater for them. However, this is a very big if because many adolescents still delay seeking professional help when they become pregnant. This is especially true for the younger ones who are less able to accept the fact that they might be pregnant. This problem can only be overcome if the educational system does a better job of teaching the facts of pregnancy to adolescents. There is also a need to provide nutritional guidance to adolescent mothers particularly those coming from lower socio-economic levels. However, it is not sufficient to focus only on the nutritional and other health aspects, for it is essential that the emotional problems facing the pregnant teenager be acknowledged. For some adolescents these emotional problems may be so great as to inhibit their being able to implement adequate health care practises.

Although much has been written about the nutritional deficiencies of adolescent mothers, less attention has been paid to other maternal factors affecting the health of the infant. For example, an increasing number of teenage girls are smoking; yet many are unaware of the detrimental effects smoking has on the fetus as well as on the young child after it is born. Alcohol and other drugs can also have serious effects on the development of the fetus and adolescents need to be warned about these potential dangers. Unfortunately, many teenagers are not aware of the symptoms of pregnancy and by the time they become aware of their pregnancy, heavy smoking and/or drinking will already have had an effect.

The children of unmarried mothers experience more illnesses than the children of married mothers. In the Nova Scotia study (Mac-Donnell, 1981) these children were more likely to have been hospitalized and to have been hospitalized with serious health ailments. Low levels of education and poverty were strongly associated with this greater incidence of hospitalization. Inadequate housing was also a contributing factor as several of the mothers lived in accommodations which were poorly heated and drafty.

Teenage parenthood can affect the child's intellectual and social development. Dryfoos and Belmont (1979) found a relationship between maternal age level and I.Q. such that the younger the mother's age at the child's birth the lower the child's I.Q. was likely to be. Also, children whose mothers had low educational levels had lower I.Q. levels. Similarly, in a study of 50 teenage mothers in Toronto, the older teenage mothers were more likely to have brighter children (Sacks et al., 1982). Also, those mothers who reported having close relations with their family had children with higher developmental quotient scores. Sacks et al. suggest that having a close relationship with the family is an indication that the family members participate in the child's care and provide additional stimulation. Also the emotional support received by the mother may help to improve her own parenting skills.

In a longitudinal study of children of adolescent childbearers it was found that when these children became teenagers they had lower educational aspirations and were less sociable. There was a definite tendency for children of adolescent parents to repeat the early marriage, early parenthood and higher fertility cycle of their parents (Card, 1978).

There is strong evidence that adolescent mothers provide less intellectual encouragement and are low in verbal interaction with their infants (Phipps-Yonas, 1980). These interactions are critical in the social-psychological development of the infant. Phipps-Yonas suggests that problems in childrearing arise because teenage girls often know very little about infants and parenting. This ignorance when combined with immaturity and higher levels of stress can result in inadequate mothering.

Consequences for the Mother

For an adolescent, having a baby tends to have serious educational and economic consequences. A national study was done in the United States which matched samples of young people for socio-economic status and educational expectations at age 15. When re-interviewed at age 29, mothers who had given birth before they were 18 were only half as likely to have graduated from high school as those who had postponed childrearing until they turned 20. The impact on college education was even more significant as women who had delayed childbearing until their twenties were four to five times more likley to have completed college than those who became mothers in their teens (Alan Guttmacher Institute, 1981).

In a study of teenage mothers in Toronto, Sacks et al., (1982) found that most of the teenagers had low educational aspirations even before their pregnancy. After the pregnancy most (78%) were not continuing their schooling. Low levels of education severely limit future employment opportunities. Thus most of the mothers who worked had unskilled or semi-skilled jobs. Childbearing responsibilities may further limit employment possibilities. Not surprisingly then the economic costs of adolescent pregnancy are very high. In both the Toronto and Nova Scotia studies the most common problem mentioned by the mothers was "getting enough money to meet expenses".

Adolescents who are mothers are far more likely to be on welfare than adolescents who do not have children. In the Nova Scotia study more than one-half of the teenage mothers had relied upon some form of government financial aid. In the study of 87 single teenage mothers in Ontario, 85% were on social assistance throughout the first 18 months after the birth of the baby and most turned to Ontario Housing for housing assistance (MacKay & Austin, 1983). This presents a considerable economic cost to society not only in terms of direct welfare benefits but also in terms of the many health and social services required by this group.

There is a high degree of residential instability among unmarried mothers. In the Nova Scotia study nearly 60% had changed places of residence at least once during the 18 month study period. The main reason was that because of limited finances, they could only afford the poorest quality of accommodations and many often moved trying to get better living accommodations. Nearly 40% of the unmarried mothers were judged by the interviewers to have housing problems.

The poor economic situation of many adolescent mothers is intensified by the fact that they are likely to have more children than women who wait until they are at least age 20 to begin childbearing. Women who have their first birth while under the age of 18 have about 46% more children than those who wait until the middle to late twenties to give birth (Alan Guttmacher Institute, 1981).

In addition to greater economic problems adolescent mothers are more likely to face social and recreational problems. In the Nova Scotia study mothers living alone with their children experienced considerable problems with loneliness and isolation. They had more problems obtaining satisfactory babysitters and participated in recreational activities less often than mothers with other living arrangements.

Despite their many problems, most adolescent mothers seem relatively content with their role as mothers and fairly happy with their life situations (Sacks et al., 1982). In the Toronto study almost all of the teenagers said they really enjoyed being a mother and that they never regretted the decision to keep the child. In the Nova Scotia study about half the mothers indicated they were happy with their life. Yet almost all of these mothers said that given the difficulty of unmarried parenthood they would advise other young single women to seriously consider the negative consequences of pregnancy and to take precautions accordingly.

The extended family often plays a key role in the success or failure of an adolescent mother's adapting to parenthood. Furstenberg (1976) in a five year follow-up study of teenage mothers found that the support provided by families was significant in helping adolescents to achieve their educational goals, secure employment and manage well as a parent. Furstenberg found that the typical reaction of parents to their daughter's pregnancy was shock and dismay. Most had not accepted the idea that their daughter might be sexually active and many were not informed about the pregnancy until late into the second or even third trimester. Parents were also often excluded from the daughter's decision making process regarding whether or not she should keep the baby. In the Toronto study about one-half of the parents did not want their daughter to keep the baby. Despite this most parents felt some obligation to assist the daughter with taking care of the child.

A high proportion of teenagers choose to remain with one or both parents. In the Toronto study by Sacks, one-half of the mothers with children three years of age or older were living with one or both of their parents. Young mothers who stay with their families tend to be better off and are likely to have children with fewer developmental problems (Furstenberg, 1976).

A study by Mednick et al. (1979) showed that the physical health of children born to adolescent mothers was better if the mother and child lived in the same household as the grandmother. Also a teenager living with her mother was more likely to either continue with her schooling or to be employed. Not only could the grandmother provide day care, she could also help to raise the quality of infant care. Furstenberg also found that mothers receiving substantial help from their family in the raising of their children were more likely to express positive views about their offspring and less likely to report behavioural problems.

There can also be negative consequences on family relationships. Furstenberg reported that some daughters found it difficult to eventually leave their parents because they had become so dependent upon them to assist with childrearing. Other problems may arise because of disagreements over childrearing practices especially discipline.

Teenage mothers are more likely to receive financial assistance from their family if they live with their relatives. If they move out of the parental household they loose the value of free or subsidized room and board as well as lessening the chances of a relative being available to provide day care. Furstenberg found that a significant number of women came back to their families after a broken marriage. In several of these cases families were not willing to provide assistance until the daughter had separated from her husband.

In summary, unwed adolescent mothers are at a disadvantage. Most have responsibility for a child without much support from the father and with limited educational and financial resources of their own. The situation often places severe limitation on the final education and occupational attainments of these young women. If subsequent pregnancies occur soon after the first, there is further strain on their resources and ability to cope.

Many of the problems in adolescent pregnancy are related to low socio-economic status. Teenage mothers from advantageous socioeconomic and family backgrounds are more likely to overcome their difficulties. Most support received by the young mothers is supplied by their nuclear families and the availability of material and emotional support is greater when the adolescents remain in the home. The assistance offered by family members significantly alters the life chances of young mothers, enhancing their prospects of educational achievement and economic advancement and contributing to the well-being of their children.

The Male Role

Because it is the female who becomes pregnant most of the attention is focused on her and the male partner is often ignored. Unfortunately little research has been done on teenage fathers. A typical stereotype is that of the uncaring male, who claims no responsibility for the child. In actual fact, most males are concerned about the possibility of their girl friend becoming pregnant. Of the sexually active males in our study of high school and university students, about three-quarters said that they had worried at sometime about the possibility of their partner becoming pregnant. An interesting difference between males and females was found in response to the question of what they would do in the event of pregnancy. More males (46%) than females (28%) said they preferred to get married if a pregnancy were to occur.

Male decision-making is strongly influenced by the type of relationship with the partner. If pregnancy were to occur with a casual dating partner most males would prefer abortion or adoption; whereas, with a steady dating partner most prefer marriage or the girl keeping the baby herself (Redmond, 1982).

Comparatively few males, in fact, do get married as a consequence of pregnancy. For those who do get married the dissolution rate is two to three times that for marriages occurring after age twenty (Alan Guttmacher Institute, 1981). For the most part the fathers are young and have limited schooling; consequently, their economic prospects are poor and few can provide adequate means of support for the child. The number of fathers maintaining contact with their children quickly declines with increasing age so that after two years very few fathers see their children anymore (Furstenberg, 1976).

In the Halifax study about one-third of the mothers married the father of the child or were living in a common-law relationship with him. Of those not living with the child's father most received no financial assistance from him. Even when assistance was obtained it was quite small. About half of the fathers who were not living with the child's mother took some interest in their child although only a minority had an extensive interest. In a study of 87 adolescent mothers in Ontario two-thirds of the fathers had not visited the child in the previous four weeks (MacKay & Austin, 1983).

In the Toronto study only 14% of the mothers married the child's father. Ten percent of the mothers named their husband or common-law spouse as providing close emotional support while 40% named their current boy friend. Only 38% had received financial assistance from the child's father.

While the father may provide economic and/or emotional support to the teenage mother, he may also create more problems. For example, he may not agree with the girl's decision about keeping the infant or giving it up for adoption and he may try to discourage the girl from living with her parents. He may also cause problems when the teenage mother begins dating other men.

Educational and Service Programs

There is a definite need for improved sex education including birth control education programs to reduce the number of teenage pregnancies. Statistics compiled in Ontario by Orton and Rosenblatt (1981) indicate that counties with well developed sex education and family planning service programs have had the greatest decline in teenage pregnancies.

In addition to learning about methods of contraception, adolescents should be informed about the signs and symptoms of pregnancy and of the value of having an early pregnancy test so that pre-natal care can be provided early in the pregnancy. Furthermore they should be informed about the effects that poor nutrition, smoking, alcohol and other drugs have on the developing fetus. They should also be informed of the different agencies available to provide counselling and other services.

Because most adolescent mothers are not in school, there is a need for community health and social services agencies to provide a variety of services to this group such as:

— assistance with completing education and/or job training,
— assistance in obtaining adequate housing,
— assistance in obtaining day care services particularly for infants,
— obtaining financial assistance,
— teaching child development concepts,
— teaching parenting principles including nutrition and health care.

The many difficulties faced by unmarried mothers are aggravated by conditions of social isolation from others. To overcome this, support groups of single mothers need to be developed. Not only could these groups provide emotional support but through the peer group process, the mothers would be more open to learning about how they might better develop their own parenting skills. Most importantly they could develop self-confidence regarding their parenting abilities. This is of crucial importance as it is very difficult for parents to implement effective parenting practices until they have sufficiently developed their own feelings of self-esteem and competence.

Comprehensive resource centres for teenage mothers have recently been started in Canada. Toronto has two such centres, Jessies and Humewood House. Both provide a wide variety of programs and services ranging from prenatal classes, which include parenting skills to housing replacement. These agencies are equipped with a nursery which enables the mother to take classes. An important component of these programs is improving the self-image of the mothers thus enabling them to learn parenting and other skills more effectively as well as to set goals for themselves.

Sexually Transmitted Diseases

During the 1980's sexually transmitted diseases became a focus of attention in the mass media. In particular, Canadians were presented with alarming stories on genital herpes and AIDS, sexually transmitted diseases which most people had not heard of until the 1980's. The following newspaper and magazine headlines illustrate the dramatic manner in which these stories were presented:

"The Creeping Shame of the Love Virus"
"Sex, Cancer and the Perils of Promiscuity"

"Herpes Victims Unite to Fight Leper Label"
"AIDS Victim Fights Misconceptions, Killer Infections"

Traditionally it was believed that only the veneral diseases of gonorrhea, syphillis, chancroid, lymphogranuloma venereum and granuloma inguinale, could be transmitted sexually from one person to another. However, in recent years it has become recognized that other diseases could be transmitted sexually and therefore the newer term of sexually transmitted diseases or STDs has emerged. Although genital herpes has been a focus of recent media attention, other sexually transmitted diseases have also been discussed, especially AIDS.

Incidence of STD's

We do not have accurate statistics on the incidence of STDs because physicians are not required to report all cases of sexually transmitted diseases. Even when physicians are supposed to report cases of specific diseases such as gonorrhea there is considerable under-reporting. For example, some physicians may not report cases because of concern over their patients' confidentiality. Nevertheless, there are indications that the numbers of cases of STDs, especially genital herpes are on the rise. In 1982 there were 6,224 laboratory reports of herpes virus in Canada. This was an increase of 140% over the number of herpes cases reported in 1980 (Canada Diseases Weekly Report 9, 21, 81-84, 1983).

From the early 1960's to the early 1980's the reported rate of sexually transmitted diseases among adolescents in Canada almost tripled with most of the increase occurring in the late 1960's and early 1970's. Since the early 1970's rates among 15 to 19 year old males have stayed approximately the same whereas female rates have continued to increase. (See Figure 5.) In 1982, for 15 to 19 year olds there were 4,098 cases of sexually transmitted diseases reported for males and an even greater number, 6,956 reported for females. Among 20 to 24 year olds there were 11,478 STD cases reported for males and 7,871 cases reported for females (Statistics Canada Catalogue 82-201). Almost all of the reported cases were gonorrhea. The rate of reported STDs varies considerably from one region of Canada to another. The lowest reported rates of STDs are found in the eastern provinces while the highest rates are in the western provinces and in the north. (See Table 9.)

Although it is commonly thought that teenagers contribute a disproportionate number of sexually transmitted disease cases, in actual fact, they contribute to less than 20 percent of the total reported cases.

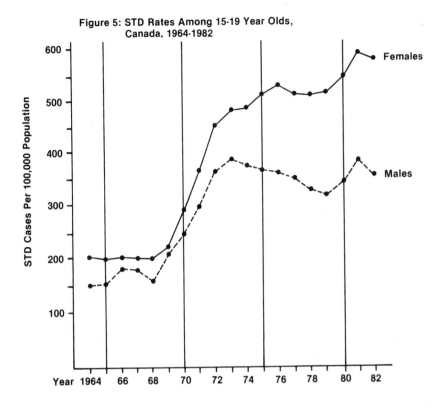

Figure 5: STD Rates Among 15-19 Year Olds,
Canada, 1964-1982

Source: Based on Statistics Canada Reports #82-201,
1964-1978 and Sexually Transitted Disease Annual
Reports 1978-1982 Health & Welfare Canada.

TABLE 9
NOTIFIABLE SEXUALLY TRANSMITTED DISEASE
AMONG 15–19 YEAR OLDS,
BY PROVINCE AND SEX, 1982.*

| | No. of Cases | | Rate per 100,000 | |
	Male	Female	Male	Female
Newfoundland	76	69	240	223
P.E.I.*	—	—	—	—
Nova Scotia	107	181	252	450
New Brunswick	7	23	19	67
Quebec	392	651	129	224
Ontario	1139	1981	283	517
Manitoba	463	696	977	1510
Saskatchewan	291	336	619	747
Alberta	864	1494	795	1458
British Columbia	488	871	409	765
Yukon	26	46	2167	460
Northwest Territories	245	237	9074	9480
Total	4098	6585	357	601

*Sexually Transmitted Disease in Canada, 1982, Annual Report, Health & Welfare Canada (unpublished).
**No data by age for P.E.I.

The highest rates of gonorrhea and genital herpes are found among those aged twenty to twenty-four.

Among those who are twenty years of age and over, cases of gonorrhea are significantly higher among males than among females, however, the opposite is true among adolescents where more females than males have gonorrhea. This difference between the ages might be explained by the fact that many young women date older males and because older males are more likely to have an STD this increases the possibility of adolescent females also contracting an STD. There is also the possibility of a higher rate of reporting for younger women because they are more likely than women over 20 years of age to attend public STD clinics, from which all cases are reported.

Increases in the STDs have paralleled changes in sexual behaviour beginning around the middle 1960's. Compared with the 1960's, young people are having sexual intercourse at younger ages and with more partners. These changes in sexual practices have greatly increased the exposure of young people to STDs. Changes in contraceptive practices have also been a factor as with the introduction of the birth control pill in the 1960's, many couples no longer use condoms which provide the best protection against certain STDs. STDs have been especially difficult to eradicate because young people are often ignorant of the symptoms and thus unaware they may have an STD. As well there is still considerable social stigma and embarrassment surrounding STDs so that young people who have symptoms may delay seeing a physician. Even more troublesome, is the fact that many carriers of STDs such as gonorrhea are asymptomatic and may spread the disease unknowingly.

Many young people mistakenly believe that STDs can only be transmitted through sexual intercourse. In fact, the diseases can also be transmitted through oral or anal sex and to persons of the same sex as well as to the opposite sex. The highest rates of STDs are found among male homosexuals who transmit the diseases through oral or anal sexual activities. Generally, homosexuals have a higher rate of STDs than heterosexuals because homosexuals tend to have a greater number of sexual partners.

Females have a greater risk of acquiring STDs than do males. For example, when exposed to an infected source, females are two to four times as likely as males to develop gonorrhea. Also, the herpes virus Type 1 has been located on the genitals of females five times more often than in males while the Type 2 virus has been located twice as often on the genitals of females (Canada Diseases Weekly Reports 9, 21, 1983).

It is important to note that the body cannot build an immunity to STDs. Thus a person can be infected a number of times and also it is possible to contract more than one STD at the same time. There is disagreement about the extent to which one can contract an STD from objects such as toilet seats or wet towels. Nevertheless, even physicians who believe it is possible to contract an STD from objects such as toilet seats agree that the possibilities are remote in comparison to the possibility of obtaining an STD from an infected person.

The Most Common STDs

The common STDs in Canada in the order of their occurrence are: non-gonococcal urethritis, gonorrhea, venereal warts, candidiasis, trichomoniasis, genital herpes, and syphilis. Of these, young people are most concerned about genital herpes and this is not surprising because of the considerable publicity given to this STD.

Genital Herpes

There are two types of herpes viruses: Type 1 which usually appears in the mouth as cold sores and Type 2 which usually appears in the genital region. Among males, Type 1 seldom appears on the genitals whereas among females Type 1 occurs on the genitals in a significant proportion of cases. (Canada Diseases Weekly Reports, 9, 21, 81-84; 1983.)

The main symptoms are tiny fluid-filled blisters which usually appear within 2 to 20 days after sexual contact. When the blisters break open they change into painful ulcers which may be accompanied by swollen lymph glands, muscle aches and sometimes fever. The initial symptoms are a tingling or itching sensation with first attacks averaging about three weeks. Recurrent infections tend to be milder and of less duration than the initial infection.

There is a high misdiagnosis for herpes. In a study of 100 people with genital herpes Cuthbert (1981) found 33% had received other diagnoses, with the most prevalent being yeast infection or syphilis. Cuthbert states that this misdiagnosis is not surprising because a high proportion of physicians do not use viral cultures to test for herpes.

The main medical problem with herpes is that it is a painful nuisance. Generally, females experience a greater degree of pain and distress than males. In one American study 67% of the males compared with 39% of the females reported that during recurring episodes lesions were either painless or mildly painful (Knox et al., 1982).

A relationship has been established between invasive genital herpes and cancer of the cervix, however, the possibility of developing cancer can be considerably reduced through regular pap tests. There is also the possibility that a woman with active herpes may pass this on to an infant during delivery but this danger can be overcome by having a caesarian section at birth.

For people with genital herpes the most distressing aspects are that there is no cure and recurring infections are unpredictable. Among Cuthbert's (1981) subjects recurrent outbreaks were frequent with 43% reporting monthly outbreaks and 22% reporting every other month. Similarly, in an American study about two-thirds had five or more episodes of genital herpes annually (Knox et al., 1982).

There is disagreement about whether or not herpes can be transmitted during its dormant phase. Some health professionals believe that virus excretion can occur in a few cases even in the absence of lesions (Cuthbert, 1981).

Most people react with considerable emotional upset upon discovering they have genital herpes. Given the widespread negative publicity about herpes by the media, it is not surprising that some people have an almost hysterical attitude toward it. Psychological reactions found by Cuthbert include shock, denial, anger, guilt, fear, alienation, shame, embarrassment, depression and low self-esteem. Cuthbert reports that shock is most often the initial response in that none of the subjects anticipated contracting herpes. Cuthbert notes that "shock is particularly intense for those people who are unaware either that their partner had herpes or that the disease could be transmitted through oral-genital sex" (p. 35). In Cuthbert's study, 90% of the herpes patients said they did not know their partner had herpes and 74% said the person did not have symptoms of herpes. Only about half (57%) of the herpes patients said they would tell a new sex partner they had herpes.

Anger is directed toward oneself, the sexual partner and the physician. Many feel guilty because they assumed that only "bad" people get herpes. There is also fear of passing the disease to others as well as the fear of being rejected and condemned by others. One of the most difficult decisions is whether or not to inform potential sex partners and if so at what stage in a relationship. Because the emotional stress associated with herpes can be so great, those having herpes need to develop positive means of coping with the disease. This is especially true since emotional stress can trigger further recurrences. To assist people with herpes in coping with the disease, self-help groups have emerged to provide emotional support and accurate information. In Canada the main group is REACH, Box 70, Station B, Toronto, Ontario.

Genital herpes may be a potent force in slowing down the sexual revolution. Many young people are terrified of contracting herpes and this has led some to re-evaluate the idea of engaging in casual sexual relationships. In the American study by Knox et al. (1982) 25% of patients with genital herpes said that herpes contributed to the breakup of a longstanding relationship and 21% had been rejected by a potential sex partner due to herpes. Ten percent of the patients with herpes said they had ceased sexual activity altogether and one percent limited sexual involvement only to other persons with herpes (STD Bulletin, 1982, 2(1). In another study of herpes patients Eder (1982) found that herpes increased sexual problems such as impotency and decreased the frequency of sexual relations.

Although at present there is no cure for gential herpes, scientists are following several promising leads and it is possible that a cure will be found in the near future. At present the antiviral agent acyclovir can be used to diminish the symptoms at the first occurrence.

Gonorrhea

Gonorrhea is caused by the gonococcus bacterium which lives in warm, moist membranes. Transmission can occur through vaginal intercourse and through oral or anal intercourse. Most males will exhibit symptoms within three to eight days after infection with the main symptoms being frequent urination with pain or burning sensations. Often there is a penile discharge. Most women do not exhibit symptoms, although for those who do the most common is a yellow-green discharge. If left untreated gonorrhea can invade the reproductive system of both males and females and cause sterility. The preferred treatment is penicillin. For penicillin resistant gonorrhea spectinomycin is usually effective. In 1981 there were 33 reported cases of penicillin resistant gonorrhea in Canada many of which originated from contacts in Asia. (Sexually Transmitted Disease Annual Report, 1981, National Health & Welfare.)

Non-Gonococcal Urethritis (NGU)

NGU is one of the most common STDs. It is an irritation of the urethra diagnosed mainly in males. Women may act as carriers. Basically it refers to any inflammation of the urethra which is not caused by gonorrhea. The symptoms are similar to those of gonorrhea but are less severe than with gonorrhea. NGU may have several different causes including different kinds of bacteria such as the chlamydia organism. Chemical irritation caused by vaginal sprays or vaginal contraceptives can also result in NGU. Treatment is usually with tetracycline.

Syphilis.

Syphilis is caused by a thin, corkscrew-like bacterium transmitted through all forms of sexual contact. In primary syphilis a painless sore or chancre develops at the transmission site. It is often unnoticed. During the secondary phase the most common symptom is a painless rash on the body which does not cause itching. There may be headaches or backaches and loss of hair. During the latency stage when there are not visible external symptoms, severe damage to body organs and possibly death may result. Treatment is with antibiotics. Rates of syphilis have declined over the last several years except for homosexual males.

Venereal Warts

Venereal warts are warts on the genital organs caused by a virus. They may appear weeks or even months after sexual contact with an infected partner. Treatment is by chemicals or surgery to remove them. They may re-occur at the same site.

Candidiasis

Candidiasis is a yeast infection caused by the fungus candida albicans. This fungus is normally found in the vagina and in the large intestine of men and women. Irritation results when the fungus overmultiplies. This may result from pregnancy, diabetes, birth-control pills, antibiotic treatment and lowered resistance. In females the most common symptoms are a burning, itching in the vagina and a cheese-like vaginal discharge. In men there may be an irritation of the penis and possibly urethritis. Treatment is by prescription suppositories or ointments.

Trichomoniasis

Trichomoniasis is an infection caused by contact with the vaginal or uretheral discharges of infected persons. The usual symptom is a greenish-yellow or white foamy vaginal discharge that has an unpleasant odour. The vulva may become painful and itchy. The infection can be transmitted sexually but also through contact with moist objects such as towels or toilet seats. Most males are asymptomatic but may be carriers.

Other STDs

There are several other diseases which can be transmitted sexually including pubic lice, scabies, cystitis (bladder infection), prostatitis (infection of the prostate), hepatitis B and parasitic intestinal infections. The latter two are more commonly found among male homosexuals.

AIDS

In 1982 the media began publicizing stories on AIDS (Acquired Immune Deficiency Syndrome) which was referred to as "the gay plague" because it was found mainly among male homosexuals.

Other groups susceptible to AIDS are Haitians, intravenous drug users and hemophiliacs. What is most frightening about this disease is its high rate of fatality. Infections in AIDS patients are extremely difficult to eradicate. Also the incidence of AIDS is doubling about every six months. As of June 24, 1983 the Laboratory Centre for Disease Control in Ottawa reported 29 confirmed cases of AIDS in Canada, 17 of which had resulted in death. None of these cases involved adolescents.

The disease breaks down the body's natural system of immunities leaving the victims susceptible to a variety of infections, such as Kaposi's sarcoma, which is a rare cancer, and pneumonia. Victims usually suffer marked weight loss and die with multiple infections. Although the cause is not known evidence suggests that AIDS is transmitted either through the blood or sexually through body secretions such as semen or saliva. While the disease has been mainly restricted to specific groups there is concern about possible widespread public contagion. This has led governments in both Canada and the United States to select AIDS as a priority issue for health research.

Pelvic Inflammatory Disease and Infertility

Increased rates of pelvic inflammatory disease (PID) and infertility have paralleled increased rates of STDs. Pelvic inflammatory disease is an infection often originating in the cervix that ascends to the upper reproductive tract. PID can lead to permanent damage to the fallopian tubes and in developed countries such as Canada 15 to 20 percent of women who develop PID become infertile (Sherris and Fox, 1983). STDs such as gonorrhea and chlamydial infections are a major source of PID-related infertility. The damage that these STDs can cause to fertility depends largely on how quickly they are treated.

Women who use an IUD for contraception are at greater risk of PID than women who use other contraceptive methods. Researchers suspect that the tail of the IUD makes it easier for bacteria to pass through the cervix, (Guilleband, J., 1978). Pill users are at less risk of PID because the pill by thickening the cervical mucus makes it more difficult for bacteria to pass through the cervix.

Reproductive problems can develop in males as untreated infections of the urethra may spread to the vas deferens and damage fertility. Fortunately in Canada this is rare since most men who have symptoms are treated promptly with antibiotics.

The human dimension of PID is aptly portrayed in the following case study described by Dr. Catterall in the medical journal *The Lancet*.

Consider the case of Sheila a 22 year-old secretary.

Sheila starts her active sex life when she is 17 with a boy she has known for several years. Her local family planning clinic puts her on a contraceptive pill. After 3 years she and her boyfriend part company. Later she meets a young man at a party and after a few weeks they have sex together. Shortly afterwards she notices that Michael, her new boyfriend, is behaving strangely, being evasive and avoiding situations that might lead to sex. Three weeks later she has colicky lower abdominal pain, slight vaginal discharge, and fever. When seen in our clinic she has an acute gonococcal PID necessitating hospital admission for antibiotic treatment and bed rest.

Michael now reappears, very concerned about Sheila's illness. He tells her that the night before having sex with her he had been to a party, got drunk, and found himself in bed with a complete stranger. When an urethral discharge and burning on urination developed he went to a clinic where gonorrhea was diagnosed. When he was also told how important it was to make sure the girls were examined and treated he did not mention Sheila. He thought he ought to talk to her but he could not bring himself to do so.

Sheila recovers and is soon free of symptoms. She leaves hospital 2 weeks later after several examinations and tests. Three weeks later the inflammation recurs and she is readmitted. Laparoscopy reveals bilateral moderately severe inflammation of the fallopian tubes and C. trachomatis is grown from her cervix. Treatment with bed rest and tetracycline enables her to go home from hospital 3 weeks later.

Sheila asks questions about the future. Will she be able to have babies? Have the germs done any real harm inside? If she has children will they be normal? What about a tubal pregnancy? Will sex now be painful in the future? Is she likely to have another attack? If the statistics are correct there is a 50% chance of relapse, since she had a mixed infection, a 1 in 3 chance of being sterile, a 25% chance of dyspareunia, and a 10% chance of an ectopic pregnancy. As Sheila says, the discomfort was bad enough, but sterility, recurrent infection, and painful intercourse are the things that preoccupy her now.

(The Lancet, February 7, 1981)

Cervical Cancer

Cervical cancer is one of the most common types of cancer among women. Many studies have found that women who begin having intercourse during the younger adolescent years are more likely to develop cervical cancer than women who delay the time of first intercourse. In a more recent study, age at the beginning of regular intercourse (defined as once a week or more) correlated more highly with the risk of developing cancer than age at first intercourse did (Swan and Brown, 1980). Also the number of sexual partners was a more important risk factor than early intercourse. In a study of British women the risk of cervical cancer was 14 times higher among women with six or more sexual partners than among women with only one partner (Harris et al., 1980). Frequency of sexual intercourse, by itself, was not associated with cancer risk. Also, the women who used barrier methods of contraception had a lower risk of cancer than users of other methods.

Prevention of STDs

In order to reduce the incidence of STDs among young people it is important that educators not only present factual information about STDs but also deal with the attitudinal and motivational factors inhibiting the prevention of STDs. Too often the emphasis in STD education is on detailed memorization of factual material regarding the biological aspects of STDs. Much of this information is irrelevant for STD prevention and is quickly forgotten by students. Emphasis should be placed instead on the negative attitudes pervading this topic because these negative attitudes inhibit young people from practising preventive measures and cause them to delay seeking medical attention if they suspect having an STD. Instead of lecturing, teachers should use such affective strategies as role playing, buzz groups and case studies. These would enable students to discuss the topic more comfortably and deal with attitudes inhibiting prevention of STDs. Yarber (1978) suggests that this educational strategy should be directed toward having students accept the following premises:

(1) Acceptance of the possibility of contracting an STD.
Despite some concerns about genital herpes, most young people do not seem deterred from having premarital sex because of fear of STDs. When young people are asked reasons for not having premarital sex, fear of STDs is seldom given as a reason. For example, in a study of sexually active youths in Saskatchewan only 13% had ever refrained from intercourse because they were afraid of contracting an STD. Females were more likely than males to have refrained from intercourse because of fearing STD (Weston, 1980). A major explanation for this is that many young people think that getting an STD is something that could never happen to them. Many believe that this can only happen to others and not themselves. It needs to be stressed that anyone who is sexually active faces the risk of contracting an STD.

(2) Acceptance of the fact that a person is sick, not bad, if he/she contracts an STD.
Young people are often reluctant to seek medical care if they have symptoms of an STD. They are especially worried that health professionals might pass moral judgement upon them. They need to be reassured that health professionals are trained to deal with STDs as with other illnesses and that their concern is with the health aspects.

(3) Acceptance of discriminatory sexual behaviour.
The best preventive measure against STDs is to limit one's sexual contacts. People who engage in casual sexual affairs with many dif-

ferent partners are far more likely to contract a sexually transmitted disease than those who limit their sexual activity to long-term committed relationships. This point can be most effectively made with young people if they are not "preached at."

(4) Acceptance of using preventive measures.
Having students accept preventive STD measures can be a difficult task. Many of the same factors which deter contraceptive use also inhibit preventive STD measures. Certainly for young people who believe that sex should be spontaneous and/or feel guilty about having sex preventive measures are difficult to take. Negative attitudes towards contraceptive devices are also an important constraint. Such attitudes must be dealt with realistically if preventive measures are to be encouraged. Thus STD education must include a discussion of sexual attitudes.

Use of certain contraceptive devices can reduce the transmission of STDs. The condom is one of the most effective methods of STD prevention because it acts as a physical barrier to prevent the spread of infection from one sex partner to another. In one study men who used condoms regularly were one-tenth as likely to contract gonorrhea or syphilis as men who did not use condoms (Barlow, 1977). Some vaginal spermicides and the diaphragm also provide protection.

Before having sexual relations with a new partner it is advisable to examine him or her for possible STD signs. For example, if the partner has noticeable discharge from either the vagina or penis or if there are sores or red patches on the genitals, intercourse should be avoided. Some health professionals recommend washing of the genitals with soap and water before and after intercourse. Another precaution is to urinate after intercourse because the acidity of urine provides an environment hostile to gonocci and the urine may flush out any bacteria that have entered the urethra.

(5) Acceptance of responsibility to secure medical care for persons who suspects he/she is infected.
The importance of seeking prompt medical attention whenever one suspects he or she may have contracted an STD must be emphasized. Young people should be informed that most Canadian cities have free government treatment clinics where names are kept strictly confidential. Information on these clinics can be obtained through the local public health department. Adolescents should also be informed about provincial laws regarding the treatment of minors. In Newfoundland, Prince Edward Island, Saskatchewan, and Ontario anyone sixteen years of age or older can be treated without parental permission. In

Quebec the age is 14, in New Brunswick it is 19. Manitoba, Alberta and British Columbia do not have age of consent legislation.

(6) Acceptance of responsibility for others which includes not transmitting an STD to someone and the naming of sexual partners.
The humanitarian aspect of not engaging in sexual relations if one suspects he or she has an STD needs to be stressed. Also, one's sexual partners should be contacted and encouraged to have an examination in case they have contracted the disease.

Resources

Additional information regarding the detailed clinical aspects of STDs may be obtained from public health units, STD clinics, provincial ministries of health and the Health Promotion Directorate, National Health and Welfare. A multi-media teaching kit on STDs is available from the Communication Branch of the Ontario Ministry of Health. Some cities such as Vancouver have STD hotlines where information can be obtained by telephone.

Premarital Sex and Parents

Dear Ann Landers:

We have two daughters, one is 18, the other 16. I have always main-tained good communication with my girls and we've discussed sex on many occasions. I do not believe in sex without marriage and they led me to believe they agreed. The 18-year-old felt quite strongly about remaining a virgin until marriage—even though she's been dating a young man steadily for a year.

Three months ago I was shocked to learn that the 18-year-old is having sex with her boyfriend. My feelings of disappointment and anger run very deep. Although I still don't approve of her behaviour, I'm trying to maintain the same relationship with her that existed before.

Both my husband and I hate the fact that she has been sneaking around and lying to us. I especially feel betrayed and have opened my mouth a few times when I should have kept it shut.

Recently I tried to discuss pregnancy and birth control with her but she said she didn't want to talk about it—at least not with me. Should I just drop the subject—or keep trying?

My husband and I have done our best to bring up our daughters with values and morals, but it appears we have been failures. I am—Heartsick and Looking for Consolation.

(Guelph Daily Mercury, June, 1979)

This letter to Ann Landers illustrates the generation gap in sexual attitudes between many parents and their adolescent sons and daughters. Because many young people believe their parents' view of sexual morality differ from their own, most do not inform parents of their sexual experience. Eighty percent of the sexually experienced males and 72% of the females in our research had not told their parents about having had intercourse. Of those who told their parents, the males usually told both parents whereas females told mothers more than fathers. A university female commented:

I wish I could be honest with my parents but knowing how disappointed they would be always stops me.

Young people whose parents had university education were more likely to inform their parents than those whose parents had less than grade 8 education. Generally, higher educated parents are more accepting of premarital sex than are parents with less education. Of the females whose parents disapproved of premarital sex, only 8% had told their parents as compared with one-half whose parents approved of premarital sex. Among males, only 5% of those with parents disapproving of premarital sex told their parents compared with 36% whose parents approved of premarital sex. There was also a strong relationship between length of sexual experience and having told parents with parents more likely to be informed if their son or daughter had been engaging in intercourse since the early teenage years.

In another study of 200 university women, we asked the extent to which they discussed specific sexual topics with their parents (Herold & Way, 1983). The topic most commonly discussed with both parents was attitudes toward premarital sex with 80% having discussed this with their mothers and 55% having discussed this with their fathers. Another topic commonly discussed was contraception with 70% having discussed this with their mothers and 29% with fathers. However, for most the discussion was on a general level and specific instructions on contraceptive use were rarely given. Discussion involving more intimate topics was usually avoided. Only 15% had ever discussed such topics as oral sex, masturbation or sexual thoughts with their mothers and only 2% had discussed these topics with their fathers. Even fewer (9%) had discussed sexual techniques with their mothers and less than one percent had ever discussed this with their fathers. When discussions did take place, they were on a very general level with personal details seldom being given.

With my mother I've talked about the entire issue of premarital sex and living together, in general, but I've never directly stated that I am having sex.

Why are most parents uninformed about their son's or daughter's sexual behaviour? To answer this question we need first to look at sex education in the home. Beginning in early childhood most children are brought up with the idea that sex is something to be kept hidden from others. Many parents hesitate about introducing sex education to their children and instead wait for their children to bring up the subject. Parents often believe that to provide information before the child is ready might result in developmental problems. However, children may have problems asking the right questions and find it difficult to ask questions about sex if they are not encouraged to do so. This reinforces in parents the belief their children are not interested in learning about sexuality and provides a rationale for not discussing the subject. Then typically what happens is the parents keep putting off discussion believing the child is too young. By the time the child reaches puberty it is already too late because both parents and child have become so conditioned to not discussing sexual issues that it is almost impossible to reverse the process. Not surprisingly then, young people commonly turn to their peer group for information. A university female commented:

I remember my parents discouraging sex talk at home. Even in cases where I had important questions to ask, only brief, vague answers were supplied and incorrect or substitute language was used instead of the correct terms. As a result, I found it very embarrassing and difficult to discuss sexual matters with my family.

Some parents find it difficult to discuss even the basic reproductive facts with their children. A high school girl commented:

Just before I reached puberty, my mother came to me one day and suggested we go in my room and have a little 'talk'. We sat down and I felt truly embarrassed, my mother was flushed and seemed nervous, and I was nervous because I knew what the talk was to be about. My mother quickly rhymed off the use of Kotex and gave me a booklet and told me to read it. Then she left. That was my entire "sex education" in the home.

Parents sometimes lack adequate knowledge to answer their children's questions. In a survey of parents in Prince Edward Island, MacLeod (1980) found considerable lack of knowledge about methods of birth control. Many were even misinformed about the methods they were currently using. In a survey of 130 mothers with children in grades 6, 9, and 12, Joan Marsman (1983) found that 42% were uncertain about whether they were giving their child accurate information about sex. Almost one-half (47%) were not sure at times what to tell their child about sex. Parents may be uncertain about the values they hold and not know what to believe themselves.

Often parents are reluctant to provide sex education because of their own lack of sex education when they were growing up. In Marsman's survey only 20% of mothers said the sex education provided by their own parents was satisfactory and 75% wished their parents had talked more to them about sex.

A few parents worry that by discussing sexual matters with their children they may encourage sexual experimentation. Yet research suggests the opposite, namely that when parents have good communication about sex with their children, their children are more likely to delay the age of their first intercourse experience.

Some parents would like to assume greater responsibility in the sex education of their children but find it difficult to do so. Although many parents are uncomfortable discussing sex education topics with their children, few can admit this. Only 12% of Calgary high school students thought that parents find it easy to talk to their teenagers about contraception (Meikle et al., 1980). It would be helpful for parents to realize that their children would be accepting of the parents' saying "I am uncomfortable discussing this with you."

The manner in which parents touch the child and demonstrate their affection as well as their attitude about the body and physiological development affect a child's sexual perspective. As a result of negative conditioning, many young people have problems relating to breast examination, internal pelvic examinations and the use of birth control devices. Some young people are so severely handicapped by negative parental conditioning regarding sexuality that they find it extremely difficult to function sexually in their later adult life.

A university female commented:

As far back as I can remember I have felt very confused and uncomfortable with the concept of sex. My parents had always been very private about sex and as a result I grew up with the idea that anything to do with sex was dirty and not to be discussed. Whenever I asked a question about my body or inquired where babies came from, I was hurriedly given some partial explanation, or informed that I would learn at some later date. This type of reply led me to believe that there was something mysterious about the human body that I shouldn't know and shouldn't want to know. I began to feel guilty about my curiosity and embarrassed about the unspeakable parts of my body. I wasn't sure why there was so much secrecy, but I quickly learned that it wasn't an acceptable topic to discuss with your family or anyone else.

As I was growing up I was never exposed to proper sexual terminology in my home. When, in health classes we began to learn that these un-mentionable parts had names, I shuddered at the thought of using them. Despite the passage of time, and my increasing comfort with sexuality, I still to this date find it difficult to use the correct terms.

The sex education of boys is usually more neglected than that for girls. One reason for this is that sex education is usually left up to the mother and mothers are more uncomfortable talking about sex to sons. Marsman (1983) found that of 13 sex education topics, mothers were the most uncomfortable with discussing the subject of wet dreams with their child.

Parents usually are unaware of the needless anxieties they cause when they do not answer their children's questions about reproduc-tion and sexuality. In situations where boys have not been prepared for wet dreams and girls have not been prepared for menstruation, their first episode may be needlessly traumatic. A high school male stated:

When I had my first wet dream I was really scared because I thought that something was wrong with me. No one had ever discussed this with me, not even my friends. Luckily I discovered a sex education book and learned from it that wet dreams were a normal occurrence for teenage boys. I was greatly relieved when I read this and no longer worried about having wet dreams. I was glad I came across that book because I was too embarrassed to discuss this with my parents.

A high school female stated:

Although my mother had once told me that when I would get older I would start bleeding, I was not really prepared for my first menstruation and found it to be traumatic. I had no idea what was happening and was afraid to ask someone because I thought something "dirty" was happening to me.

In many families the only sex education adolescents receive is a vague warning against "doing it". Adolescent girls, when they begin to start dating, might be told "be careful" or "you have to watch boys because they are out to get as much as they can." Usually the meanings of these warnings are not clearly defined.

They told me it was not healthy to see one boy so frequently, made disapproving remarks regarding teenage sex and gave vaguely worded hopes that I could be "trusted". The latter technique greatly increased my degree of sexual guilt.

When I first began to date boys, I would often go home upset because the boy would want to engage in forms of sexual activities such as petting. But I always felt that it was wrong. I could never go home and talk to my mother about this because we had no communication whatsoever when it came to sexual matters.

Fathers are more embarrassed discussing sexual topics with their children than are mothers. In many families the mother is closer to the children and this makes it easier for the mother to communicate about personal topics such as sexuality.

Despite a greater acceptance of premarital sex today than previously, many parents are still opposed to premarital sex. In the study of Wellington County mothers, 61% disapproved of premarital sex for 18 year olds who were in love. The mothers were equally disapproving for males as well as for females (Marsman, 1983). In a 1975 Gallup Poll survey, parents with teenagers living at home were far less approving of premarital sex than parents not having teenagers living at home.

Parents often oppose premarital sex because they believe it might cause personal unhappiness for their children, especially for their daughters. They are concerned that if their daughter engages in premarital sex she might become a less desirable marriage partner. There is also concern over maintaining the social reputation of the family and the fear of pregnancy. In some families virginity is stressed to such an extent that it becomes a prized possession upon which the girl's whole selfhood depends.

Fathers sometimes give the impression they are more opposed to premarital sex than are mothers. Consequently fathers are often overprotective as they fear the potential loss of their daughter's reputation.

This can have a powerful impact on the daughter's attitudes regarding males and sexuality. One high school female stated:

The only thing my father ever said to me about sex was that he would not speak to us if he ever found out we were having intercourse.

Comments from university females were:

My father said that if I ever became pregnant before marriage he would disown me completely. His attitude left a lasting impression and it strongly affected my own attitudes toward premarital sex.

When I started dating my father's attitude was that all teenage boys were after just one thing—to get every girl they could into bed with them and take "advantage" of her.

Some parents are so overprotective that they try to control completely the teenager's dating life. This usually causes tremendous resentment and hostility on the part of the teenager. One university female commented:

For me one of the best things about coming to university was living away from my parents and their oppressive control of my social life. It was a tremendous feeling to know that I was no longer responsible to my parents for my sexual life. I very much resented my parents for their interference in my sexual development which I felt was my responsibility and not theirs.

Concerning sons, a worry of some fathers is the possibility of their son's becoming homosexual. Media attention to the topic of homosexuality has raised parental consiousness regarding this topic. Many fathers purposely inhibit affection toward sons because of the fear that too much affection might result in homosexuality.

Teenagers who perceive parents as disapproving of premarital sex commonly develop strategies to evade parental disapproval. One strategy is to avoid disagreeing with parental sexual attitudes. When parental views are not challenged, parents may assume their teenagers support these views. Another tactic is to avoid discussing sexual behaviour. Here the teenagers might pretend sexuality is not of interest to them. They might also keep specific information away from parents such as details of situations where they might have been alone in the house with their dating partner. Thus many parents cannot imagine their children as sexually active. Because in most families it is generally accepted that one's personal sexuality should be hidden, it is easy for teenagers to avoid discussion of their sexual behaviour with parents. This lack of communication can make it easier for parents to cope with their teenager's sexuality. Even though parents may suspect their teenagers are engaging in sexual behaviour, bringing this suspicion in the open might cause too much tension and conflict. In supporting the secrecy of teenagers, parents find it easier to cope. Given a situation where parental and teenagers' views are opposed, communication about sexuality could bring about conflict and thus non-communication maintains the harmony of the family.

Because parents generally keep their sexual behaviour hidden from children, teenagers find it difficult to imagine their parents ever engaging in sexual activity. This can inhibit discussion because parents may fear having to reveal they themselves are sexually active. However, it is not essential that adolescents and parents be totally open with one another. Most people usually feel the need to keep some aspects of their lives as private.

The effect of adolescent sexual development on parents has not been adequately explored. The sexuality of the parents themselves may be brought into greater awareness with the realization that their children have reached sexual maturity. How parents think and feel about their own bodies and sexuality will strongly influence how they respond to the developing sexuality of their children. Especially at puberty parents may introduce a distance between themselves and their teenagers in order to inhibit the arousal of sexual feelings. Few parents are comfortable discussing these feelings and they may develop guilt feelings as a result of them. In other families parents may be jealous of the sexual freedom their teenagers have and envious that they did not have this freedom when they were teenagers. Parents who have a poor sexual relationship may be reminded of this by their developing son's or daughter's sexuality and this may trigger hostility.

Although most parents have difficulty communicating with their children about sexuality, some parents are open with their children and accept their children's developing sexuality. These parents typically tend to be comfortable with their own bodies and their own sexuality. Evidence suggests that children raised by these types of parents are more likely to develop a strong sense of self-esteem and are less likely to have sexual problems later in life.

There is a definite need to offer sex education courses for parents so they could feel more comfortable and knowledgeable about answering their children's questions. Marsman (1983) found that two-thirds of mothers believed parents would benefit from a sex education program for parents offered by the school. Fortunately, agencies such as school boards, family service agencies, birth control centres and Planned Parenthood groups have begun to offer such courses.

A different approach is offered by Dr. Jean-Yves Desjardins, cofounder of the Department of Sexology, University of Quebec. As Quebec's leading sex educator, Dr. Desjardins has spoken about sexuality in public lectures to more than 300,000 adults. A major aim of Dr. Desjardins is to help parents become more accepting of their own sexuality. He believes that only if parents are first comfortable with their own sexuality will they be able to communicate effectively with their children about sex.

Sex Education
in the Schools

While some people may still believe young people are better off not knowing the "facts of life", there are many tragic consequences of not properly informing young people. Consider the following:

At midnight on January 26, 1983 a 15 year old Hamilton high school student who was alone in her bedroom gave birth. She lay in bed with the baby through the night and in the morning hid the child in a garbage bag. The mother of the teenager had no idea her daughter was pregnant.

In court, the defence lawyer stated the girl had no knowledge of childbirth and did not know how her parents would react to the situation.
(The Globe and Mail, August 9, 1983)

Another example is that of a 21 year old university student who felt that because she received no sex education at home or at school, she suffered unnecessary worry and anxiety about the physical changes which she experienced during and after puberty.

My ignorance in the area of sexuality, until I reached the university level, fills me with regret, shame and a determination that my children will not be left in such an educational vacuum in this area.

Many different agencies and professional groups are involved in sex education including religious institutions, the medical profession, social service agencies and birth control groups. Nevertheless, most formal sex education takes place in the school setting.

During the 1970's many Canadian school systems began offering sex education courses. However, very few have developed comprehensive programs and as a result most young people in Canada are not receiving adequate sex education.

A 1983 national health education study of 29,000 Canadian school children ages 9, 12, and 15 showed a considerable lack of sex education (King & Robertson, 1983). Only 35% of grade 7 students knew that it was possible for a girl to get pregnant between the ages of 12 and 15. Most thought pregnancy could not happen until after age 16. Only 22% of grade 10 students knew that usually there are no early symptoms of gonorrhea in females. Only 46% knew that mothers who smoke tend to have more premature babies.

Objectives of Sex Education

What are the objectives of sex education? When sex education courses were first introduced, the emphasis was on the negative pathological aspects of sexuality. Sex was never talked about in positive terms but rather it was viewed almost as a disease which had to be cured by repression. Masturbation, for example, was seen as a filthy habit resulting in various physical and psychological illnesses. The main objective of sex education was to stamp out as much of sexual thoughts and behaviour as possible by instilling in people a tremendous amount of sexual guilt. In more recent years although the negative aspects of sexuality are still being taught, there is a trend toward examining the positive, life-enriching aspects.

Of course, we need to be concerned with unwanted pregnancy and venereal disease, and an important objective of sex education programs should be the development of sexual responsibility so these problems will be reduced. But there is more to sex education than pregnancy and venereal disease prevention. Today most mental health professionals recognize that healthy sexual functioning is important to the well-being of individuals and of marital relationships. Most people consider a satisfying sex life as important for their happiness.

What should be the goals of sex education? The first objective is the acquisition of accurate information. A good sex education program should provide students with basic facts about sexuality and clear up misconceptions.

A second objective is the development of greater self-awareness and understanding. When students acquire more information regarding sexuality, it enables them to develop greater insight into their own sexuality. This can lead to a reduction in anxieties about their own sexual development and help young people better manage their sexual problems. A university female commented:

I feel I have learned to appreciate sex as natural and healthy behaviour and not as something dirty and not to be talked about. The course has given me a better understanding of myself in this area and has helped me to answer many of the questions I have had about sex.

A third objective is to help students clarify their own value standards over sex so that they are less dependent on the standards of peers and less likely to engage in sexual relations if they do not feel ready. This should result in more satisfactory decision-making.

A fourth objective is the improvement of communication skills. It is a myth that people are open in their discussions of sex. Most of the openness is carried out in a superficial way and sex education can provide the opportunity to discuss sex in a serious manner. However, it must be emphasized that many aspects of sex are personal and private. In promoting classroom discussion on sexual issues, it is essential that educators be aware of this and refrain from attempting to impose complete self-disclosure. Students should never feel forced to divulge matters which they believe are personal and which they do not want others to know about.

The development of open communication can only occur in a classroom setting where the teacher is a warm, accepting person who respects the opinion of students. This point cannot be overemphasized. Communication cannot take place if students are afraid to express their opinions because of concern over being ridiculed by the teacher or other students. However, given a supportive atmosphere students are highly enthusiastic about being able to discuss sexual topics in a serious manner. One student commented:

I do feel more comfortable talking about sex. I think this is because now I realize I'm not the only dumb one and other people really don't know as much about it as they would like people to think they do. Also what I have learned in this course gives me more background to draw upon when discussing the topic.

Marriage counsellors report that many couples have difficulty communicating. By developing the communication skills of our students, they should be better prepared to discuss problems with their partner.

Being more knowledgeable about sexual issues, having greater self-understanding and being able to communicate more effectively can increase one's self-esteem. A very important objective of sex education is the fostering of positive feelings of self-worth. A common problem among teenagers today is that of low self-esteem which in extreme cases leads to suicide. Sex education programs by assisting students to deal with an area of their lives which many find problematic can help to make them feel better about themselves which in turn will enable them to function more successfully in society.

Another objective of sex education is the development of a toleration for those whose opinions differ from our own. Surely one of the goals of any educational program is that of respecting the opinions of others. Too often our society is divided into conflicting groups which try to impose their views on one another rather than to accept the differing views which exist. However, sex education in schools is unlikely to change fundamental values regarding sexual behaviour. Students in sex education courses indicate that their basic values and behaviour are not changed as a result of the course. This is important to stress because of the fear some people have that talking about sex encourages students to do it. In actual fact, given a peer group environment which is usually supportive of premarital sex, the teacher can play an important role in providing support to the students who do not want to engage in premarital sex.

Finally, another goal of sex education should be the increasing of communication and closeness between parents and their children. Many students who take sex education courses indicate that it provides them with the opportunity to discuss openly sexual matters with their parents for the first time and this enables them to feel closer to their parents.

Topics in Sex Education

There are many important topics in sex education. Many of these have been discussed throughout this book. Because my own research has focussed on the topics of premarital sex and birth control I am concentrating on these areas in this chapter.

Choosing A Sexual Standard

Given the conflicting values about sex in our society, choosing a sexual standard is a serious and difficult matter. Yet it is a decision which every young person has to face.

Ira Reiss (1967) has outlined four basic standards of sexual morality: abstinence, the double standard, permissiveness with affection, and permissiveness without affection.

1. The abstinence standard prohibits sexual intercourse before marriage for everyone.
2. The double standard prohibits sexual intercourse before marriage for women, but accepts it for men.
3. The permissiveness with affection standard permits sexual intercourse within a love relationship.
4. The permissiveness without affection standard allows for sexual intercourse outside of a love relationship.

Each of these sexual standards has its costs and benefits.

The abstinence code follows traditional religious and parental values so that young people adhering to this code do not have to face the turmoil of going against religious and parental beliefs. Sexual decision making is simplified in that one does not have to decide continually whether to engage or not to engage in sexual intercourse. Certainly one does not have to worry about pregnancy or sexually transmitted disease. The major cost of this code is that it might result in considerable sexual frustration as well as conflict if one's partner does not accept this code. If the code is transgressed then considerable sexual guilt would result. Because of sexual repression some people following this code may have difficulty adjusting to a sexual life later when they get married.

The double standard is theoretically rewarding to males and exploitative of women. Obviously if the code were strictly applied, then males would have a difficult time finding accessible sexual partners. Prostitutes would be about the only women available. Males accepting this code tend to categorize women into two categories: sexual or bad and non-sexual or pure. This type of belief system could cause problems in marriage when the male might have a difficult time adjusting to a sexual relationship with his wife whom he might perceive as being pure or non-sexual. Similarly, women might have a difficult time adjusting from being non-sexual to sexual.

The permissiveness with affection standard while allowing for sexual expression when in love may cause problems in terms of defining when one is in love. Decision making is difficult because the person may be uncertain about whether he or she is ready to experience intercourse. Guilt feelings can arise when the relationship with the sexual partner ends and a new relationship is started. One 19 year old woman stated:

Previously I had rationalized my sexual activity through the expectation that my first sexual partner would be my only one. With a change of partners I had feelings of guilt in that this seemed like promiscuity.

The permissiveness without affection code potentially offers great sexual excitement and the least sexual frustration. However, one has to face the possibility of being labelled promiscuous which might cause guilt feelings and lowered self-esteem. In addition to the possibility of unwanted pregnancy there is also the greatly increased probability of contracting venereal disease through casual sex contacts.

In summary, every sexual standard has its costs as well as its rewards. One of the responsibilities of sex educators should be to discuss the different sexual standards with young people and to point out the costs and benefits of each so that young people can be in a better position to make responsible decisions about their own sexual behaviour. Ultimately, the sexual standard young people choose will be affected by their own values regarding religious teachings, parental views, personal freedom, affection, and sexual pleasure.

Sex educators should be aware that many parents want them to emphasize traditional values with the abstinence code being presented as the best one for young people. On the other hand, there is not a consensus among parents with respect to how the issue of sexual standards should be presented. In a 1982 national survey, 74% of Canadians indicated that premarital sex is "not wrong at all" or wrong only "sometimes" (Bibby, 1982). When asked if an important objective of sex education should be to discourage premarital sex, only one-third of mothers in Wellington County, Ontario agreed (Marsman, 1983). Furthermore, 76% of the mothers agreed that sex education teachers should avoid preaching at youngsters.

Nevertheless, most people would agree that the majority, if not all, younger teenagers are not mature enough to handle the responsibilities involved in having sexual intercourse. Indeed, until about age 18 most young people do not have sexual intercourse either because they do not feel ready or for moral reasons. For this group it is especially important that sex educators provide support for these values. Also, educators need to stress the building of communication skills which can help these young people deal with peer and partner pressures which might lead to early sexual involvement. This would include specific examples of how to say no to such pressure. Of course, there are other alternatives to sexual intercourse such as petting or masturbation and sex educators should be prepared to present these topics in a sensitive manner.

In providing guidance about sexual decision-making sex educators should encourage young people to consider the following questions:

1. What are the views of your religion regarding premarital sex? Are you conforming with your religious ideals?
2. Are you taking your parents' values into consideration? If your decision goes against parental values how would you feel about acting contrary to them? How would you feel if your parents found out?
3. Will you feel guilty about your decision?
4. Are you being pressured by peers or your dating partner into sexual activity for which you are not ready?
5. Are you exploiting your partner or is your partner exploiting you?
6. Are you expecting too much from sex?
7. How important to you is having a sexual relationship and what does a sexual relationship mean to you?
8. Do you have trust in your dating partner and can you communicate honestly about your needs and concerns?
9. Are you prepared to use effective contraception?
10. If contraception should fail, how would you handle pregnancy?
11. Have you considered the possibility and consequences of contracting a sexually transmitted disease?

Birth Control Education

Too often educators believe that birth control education consists only of a description of the different methods of birth control. This approach ignores the many other factors influencing birth control use, especially attitudes and values. What then should be included in the ideal birth control education program?

First, young people should know about the male and female reproductive systems, especially the menstrual cycle. Unfortunately many adolescents have incorrect assumptions about the cycle of female fertility and attempt to use the old-fashioned rhythm method on a chance basis.

They need to know about the different methods of birth control and have a clear understanding of precisely how to use them. They should also be aware of the effectiveness rate and advantages and disadvantages of each method. However, educators must avoid presenting too much information and thereby overwhelming adolescents with factual detail. Given that there is no ideal contraceptive, young people need to be familiar with more than one method because they are likely to use several different methods throughout their reproductive life. Also attitudes about the different methods should be discussed because adolescents are unlikely to use methods about which they feel uncomfortable.

Teachers and clinicians must be aware of their own biases in presenting the different methods of birth control. For example, consider how you would answer the following:

Can the condom and/or foam be used effectively by adolescents?
Are IUDs safe for young women to use?
Do the benefits of the pill outweigh possible side effects?

Educators and clinicians have differing opinions regarding these and other issues in birth control. It is essential that we be aware of these biases and how they can affect our teaching or counselling. Every method of birth control has its positive aspects and these should be stressed. The best method of birth control is one that will be used consistently by the individual.

Adolescents, especially the younger ones, often are not aware of how to obtain birth control services and of the procedures involved in obtaining them. Precise information should be provided about birth control services such as clinics including their hours, location and policies regarding confidentiality. This would also include detailed information about the procedures for the internal examination. When clinics provide birth control to young people they should make certain that written instructions are provided for the use of that method and include a description of side effects plus a telephone number to call in an emergency.

Birth control education should be presented at different grade levels throughout the junior high school and high school years. This would overcome the problem of forgotten information and, even more importantly, provide continual reinforcement of responsible sexuality.

Educators are often asked: "Why is it that so many sexually active young people know about birth control but don't use it?" The answer, of course, is that many factors influence birth control use (as shown in the contraceptive model discussed in chapter eight). In order to have adequate sex education, these factors need to be addressed.

To heighten perceived susceptibility we need to make young people aware that if they have sexual intercourse there is a good possibility of their becoming pregnant unless they take preventive action. Here statistics can be used to illustrate the large number of pregnancies occurring among adolescents. Also, we need to deal with such myths as "I won't get pregnant if I do it only once or if I only have sex once in a while." In discussing perceived susceptibility we need to make young people aware of the necessity to plan ahead to use birth control. Adolescents seldom anticipate becoming sexually active and find it difficult to think rationally about birth control after they have become sexually aroused.

To increase their perceived seriousness of a pregnancy, we need to make adolescents aware of the costs of childbirth. Teenage mothers face many economic, psychological and social problems. Also their infants face greater health and social risks than infants born to older mothers. For those few teenagers who intentionally want to become pregnant we need to pay attention to the emotional needs they are trying to satisfy through pregnancy. They must be shown that having a baby would more likely increase rather than decrease their emotional problems.

In any discussion of birth control the psychological costs of using birth control need to be presented. Adolescents may be so over-whelmed by the emotional costs of contraception at the time of intercourse that they put aside consideration of the long-term costs of a possible unwanted pregnancy.

One of the major emotional costs is embarrassment in getting and using contraception. Teachers and clinicians by discussing the different methods of birth control in a comfortable manner can help to decrease student embarrassment. Young women are particularly embarrassed about the internal examination and it is important that teachers and clinicians carefully explain the procedures involved in this examination so that young people will be less fearful of it. Also when physicians are doing an internal exam, they should try to reduce feelings of embarrassment.

Underlying many of the costs involved in using contraception is sexual guilt. Many young people cannot use contraception because it would make them feel guilty about having sexual relations. We should encourage young people to accept, as a rule, that they should never have intercourse without using contraception and if they feel guilty they should not be having intercourse.

Educators can play an important role in providing a cue to action for responsible sexuality. One technique is to use a motivating film. In 1972 I produced the film "It Couldn't Happen to Me" (Viking Films) which deals with the psychological costs of using contraception and makes young people more aware of the risk of pregnancy. In producing "It Couldn't Happen to Me" I wanted to encourage birth control use among the sexually active, while at the same time supporting the views of those who did not want to have premarital sex. Indeed, adolescents viewing the film who are opposed to premarital sex state that their views have been strengthened as a result of seeing the film.

Other factors influencing contraceptive use are age and self-esteem. Sexually active younger teenagers are less likely to use birth control than are older teenagers and thus it is important to begin formal birth control education programs during the early adolescent years.

Young people with high self-esteem are less likely to be pressured into having sex when they don't want to and are more likely to use contraception if they do engage in sexual intercourse. High self-esteem teens also feel less need to become pregnant in order to satisfy unmet emotional needs. Thus wherever possible educators and counsellors should use strategies to raise the self-esteem of adolescents.

Sex education should not only be limited to teenagers. There should be education for parents so that they will feel more comfortable discussing topics such as birth control with their sons and daughters. It is easier for teenagers to be responsible for their sexuality when their parents are able to provide positive sex education.

Peer group influence could also be used to encourage responsible sexuality. For example, Family Planning Services of the City of Toronto has sponsored the development of a teenage drama group entitled "STARR" meaning Students Talking About Responsible Relationships. Through the use of dramatic role-playing this theatre group presents important decision-making aspects of sexuality and birth control. By providing a role model the actors help adolescents to feel comfortable about discussing contraception and related issues. To make the best use of techniques such as the drama group, it is essential that students have the opportunity to discuss their own feelings and reactions in a small group setting. In this way their own peer group in the classroom can be used to reinforce the concept of responsible sexuality.

Most young people find it difficult to communicate about sexuality and birth control. Sexually active couples who discuss contraception are more likely to use it. Therefore teachers should attempt to increase the communication skills of their students. Communication exercises designed to improve the sending, receiving and interpretation of verbal and non-verbal messages should be incorporated into all sex education programs. We also need to develop contraceptive assertiveness so that a young person could tell the partner that intercourse definitely would not occur unless he or she were using effective contraception.

Often educators assume that sexuality is the female's responsibility and typically females receive more sex education than males. In Saskatchewan, 83% of females indicated they had had some sex education compared with 66% of males. In particular females were twice as likely as males to be taught about menstruation (Weston, 1980).

Adolescent males need to be educated about their sexual responsibilities. Here educators could work toward instilling feelings of respect about the other person and through values clarification exercises support the value that it is wrong to use physical or emotional coercion to try to get one's partner to become involved sexually. Males have an equal responsibility in birth control and should be knowledgeable about the different methods. It is sometimes more difficult to teach males than females because males are socialized to present the image of knowing it all. Fortunately there are audio-visual and other resource materials directed specifically at males which can help the teacher to overcome some of the difficulties involved in teaching and counselling males.

Does Sex Education Cause Promiscuity?

One belief of some opponents of sex education is that sex education promotes promiscuity. The research evidence clearly does not support this belief. Instead, research has shown that sex education does not increase premarital sex but may increase the more responsible use of contraception among young people who are sexually active. For example, Zelnik & Kim (1982), in studying a large random sample of American teenagers found that those with sex education were no more likely than those who had no sex education to engage in premarital intercourse. However, those whose sex education included birth control education were less likely to become pregnant because they were using contraception. Meikle et al. (1980) found that among 15 to 18 year old Calgary high school students there was no significant difference in coital experience between those who had or had not sex education while among 13 and 14 year old girls, fewer of those with sex education had experienced coitus. In the Province of Quebec, Dr. Jean Yves Frappier (1983), in a controlled experiment with 1,100 students in grades 9 and 11 found that those students who were given sex education were not more likely to engage in sexual intercourse. However, the sex education students did acquire more knowledge and they showed a more responsible and less exploitative attitude to sexuality.

Rather than stimulating sexual behaviour, sex education programs are typically begun as a response to increases in sexual behaviour among young people.

Canadian Attitudes to Sex Education

Do Canadians approve of the teaching of sex education? In 1974 the Gallup Poll asked Canadians, "It has been suggested that a course in sex education be given to students in high school. Do you approve or disapprove?" Seventy-three percent approved. Those who approved were asked, "Would you approve or disapprove if these courses discussed birth control?" Eighty-nine percent approved. The strongest supporters were people from large communities, those who are younger and well-educated. Nevertheless, even a majority of people over 50 approved.

In a 1979 survey by the Ontario Institute for Studies in Education, 91% of adults in Ontario said the school should be involved in sex education (Livingstone & Hart, 1979). Over 50% said that sex education means more than the provision of medical or factual information on topics such as birth control and includes a fuller treatment of the social and emotional as well as the physical aspects of sex. In a survey of Calgary parents, Meikle et al. (1980) found that 81% of parents agreed that schools should teach contraception. Ninety percent of parents surveyed in Prince Edward Island agreed that birth control information should be included in family living courses (MacLeod, 1980). Sixty-nine percent of mothers in Wellington County, Ontario agreed that schools should inform teenagers about the different methods of birth control; 18% were undecided and only 1.3% disagreed (Marsman, 1983). Only 2% believed that providing teenagers with knowledge about contraception would lead to sexual experimentation.

Every survey of parents that has been done has found the great majority of parents supporting sex education in the schools. This needs to be emphasized because opponents of sex education programs time and again will say parents are opposed to sex education, when what they are really saying is that a small vociferous minority of parents are opposed to sex education. As long as parents are informed about what is being taught and are involved in curriculum design and revision, most parents will support the school system. A good example of this occurred in Halton County, Ontario in March, 1975 when the Renaissance Committee organized a parents' night featuring the film "Sexuality and Communication". The opponents of sex education had spread so many rumours about the film that the curiosity of parents was raised and several hundred attended the film showing. When parents had the opportunity to view the film, their reaction was opposite to that predicted by the Renaissance Committee. Most parents liked the film and wished they could have seen such a film when they were in high school. Rather than remaining to listen to a tirade against sex education, most parents streamed out of the exits (The Oakville Beaver, March 19, 1975). The opponents of sex education thrive in an atmosphere where lack of knowledge about a program exists and consequently many false rumours arise. The correct action is to provide adequate information to the community.

Further indication of parental support can be seen in the fact that when parents are given the opportunity to refuse permission for their child to take a sex education course, hardly any do so. In many communities, parents have been so involved in the process of program planning and curriculum review that they have requested sex education for themselves.

Attitudes of Students to Sex Education

One concern of adults is the possibility of teaching sex education before the young people are ready. However, young people have the opposite concern—that of being taught too little material presented at a time when it is too late to be of much use to them. In 1972 we surveyed attitudes of grades 10 and 12 students in Wellington County, Ontario toward family life education (Herold et al., 1974). We found the students were overwhelmingly in favour of more family life and sex education being offered in the schools. They also preferred to have the sex education topics introduced earlier than they had been. Over 80% said that at least before the end of grade 10 they wanted to know about such topics as birth control methods, masturbation and sexual response. When we presented the statement "Teenagers are better off not knowing about contraception" 90% disagreed. When we asked if information on methods of contraception leads to experimentation, almost all disagreed. The students believed that they should be provided with information about birth control and they did not believe this information would encourage sexual activity.

Principles of Sex Education

For sex education programs to be accepted and supported by parents it is essential that some basic principles regarding the school's role in sex education be established. The following are some fundamental principles which should be considered by all school boards before sex education programs are developed.

1. The primary responsibility for sex education rests with parents and the school's role is to support the parent's role.
2. School sex education programs should reflect both parental values and student needs.
3. Parents and educators should be partners in designing and implementing school sex education programs.
4. Parents who do not wish their children to be involved in sex education should have the opportunity to withdraw their children from these classes.

5. Wherever possible, sex educators should assist both parents and their children to communicate with one another.
6. Many young people do not want to become sexually involved and their views should be supported.
7. The sexual difficulties faced by young people are increased when they are not given adequate information.

Sex Research

A related development which is having a significant impact on sex education is the rapid increase in sex research. Following from the works of Kinsey and Masters and Johnson, research is being carried out into every conceivable aspect of sexuality. This research has exploded many popular myths surrounding sexuality and has helped to replace ignorance with knowledge. This new information is beneficial both in counselling people with sexual difficulties and in educating people about sexual reality. So much research is being done and so many articles and books are being published, that it is almost impossible to be up to date. What this research is demonstrating is that sexuality is not the simple matter it was once thought to be, but rather is a highly complex area of life that is influenced by numerous factors. A responsibility of sex educators and counsellors should be to keep aware of the major research developments.

Teacher Preparation

Sex education is one of the most difficult subjects to teach because there are so many conflicting attitudes and emotions about this topic. Unfortunately some administrators assume that any teacher simply because of being a man or woman is automatically qualified to teach sex education. The importance of adequate preparation for teachers of sex education cannot be over-emphasized. A particular concern of mine is that inadequately prepared teachers are less able to distinguish between value statements and statements of fact and will often state value assertions which may not have factual validity. For example, there are still many people who believe that sexual behaviour rates among young people have not significantly changed over the past twenty years. There are others who believe that women don't enjoy sex and only do it to please males. The following student comments also illustrate the consequences of inadequate teacher preparation:

> While I was in grade six, the boys were sent to shovel snow off the outdoor rink and the girls were kept indoors to observe a film on menstruation. It was terribly confusing even when all the facts were laid

down in front of me. I felt as though there was something wrong because the boys were not allowed to observe the movie. This increased my negative feelings about the topic of sexuality.

Every year the school did its duty and showed 'from girl to woman' and 'boy to man' films. No teacher ever asked us what we thought of these films or if we had any questions. At the time, I remember that viewing these films was rather a stressful experience, particularly while we all waited for the film to roll. As I look back on this now I realize that our teachers were uncomfortable too, and that this may have been transmitted to us.

There can be no doubt that a major problem in sex education is the lack of adequately prepared teachers. Fortunately many teachers recognize this deficiency and are attending courses and workshops in sex education such as the University of Guelph's conference on human sexuality which brings together more than five hundred teachers and clinicians from across Canada each year.

A related problem is the lack of adequate resource facilities. Unfortunately very few school boards have a full-time specialist in sex education. Because of this, the responsibility for developing curriculum on sex education or of providing guidance to teachers is given to a consultant who is often busy with other responsibilities and does not have the time to deal adequately with the sex education program. One of the strongest recommendations we can make for improving sex education programs is that funds and personnel be made available at the provincial level as well as at local school board levels for the development, implementation and evaluation of such programs.

Prospects

What are the prospects for sex education? I personally believe that despite some controversies sex education programs in Canada will continue to develop and grow. I am optimistic because our children need and want the information and because most parents approve of sex education. Granted, there will be some difficulties. Nevertheless, parents in the 1980's are more willing to educate their children about sexual matters than parents of previous generations. As parents become more comfortable about providing sex education for their children, they will further increase their support of sex education programs in the schools.

References

Alan Guttmacher Institute. *Teenage pregnancy: The Problem that hasn't gone away.* New York, N.Y., 1981.

Arafat, I., & Cotton, W. "Masturbation practices of males and females." *Journal of Sex Research,* 1974, 10(4), 293-307.

Badgley, R.F., Caron, D.F., & Powell, M.G. *Report of the Committee on the Operation of the Abortion Law.* Ministry of Supply and Services, Ottawa, Canada, 1977.

Barlow, D. The condom and gonorrhoea. *Lancet,* 1977, 2, 811-812.

Barrett, F.M. "Changes in attitudes toward abortion in a large population of Canadian university students between 1968 and 1978." *Canadian Journal of Public Health,* 1980a, 71(3), 195-200.

Barrett, F.M. "Sexual experience, birth control usage and sex education of unmarried Canadian university students: Changes between 1968 and 1978." *Archives of Sexual Behaviour,* 1980b, 9(5), 367-390.

Barwin, B.N. *Encare Oval: A Clinical Study.* Paper presented to International Symposium on Reproductive Health Care, Maui, Hawaii, October, 1982.

Becker, M. (Ed.) *The health belief model and personal health behaviour.* San Francisco: Society for Public Health Education, Inc., 1974.

Bell, A.P., & Weinberg, M.S. *Homosexualities: A study of diversity among men and women.* New York: Simon & Schuster, 1978.

Bell, R.R., & Coughey, K. "Premarital sexual experience among college females, 1958, 1968, and 1978." *Family Relations,* 1980, 29, 353-357.

Bibby, R.W. *The Moral Mosaic: Sexuality in the Canadian 80s.* PROJECT CAN80, Release No. 1: Sexuality. Lethbridge, Alberta: University of Lethbridge, 1982.

Black, R. "Why notify the police: The victim's decision to notify the police of an assault," *Criminology,* 1974, 11, 555-561.

Boldt, I.E.D., Roberts, L.W., & Latif, A.H. "The provision of birth control services to unwed minors: A national survey of physician attitudes and practices." *Canadian Journal of Public Health,* 1982, 73, 392.

Brown, H.G. *Sex and the single girl.* B. Geis Associates, Cleveland: World Publishing Co., 1970.

Burgess, A.W., & Holmstrom, L.L. "Rape, sexual disruption and recovery." *American Journal of Orthopsychiatry,* 1979, 49(4), 648-657.

Card, J. *Long-term consequences for children born to adolescents* (Final Report) (Contract HD-72820, National Institute of Child Health and

Human Development). American Institute for Research, Palo Alto, California, December 1978.

Carns, D.E. "Talking about sex: Notes on first coitus and the double standard." *Journal of Marriage and the Family*, 1973, 35(4), 677-688.

Catterall, R.D. "Biological Effects of Sexual Freedom." *The Lancet*, February 7, 1981, 315-319.

Christensen, H. "Normative theory derived from cross-cultural family research." *Journal of Marriage and the Family*, 1969, 31(2), 209-222.

Cowell, C.A. In *An exploration of the limitations of contraception: Proceedings of a conference*. Toronto: Ortho Pharmaceutical (Canada) Ltd., 1975, 19-26.

Crépault, C., & Gemme, R. *La Sexualité Prémaritale*. Montréal: Les Presses de l'Université du Québec, 1975.

Cuthbert, M. *The herpes handbook*. REACH, 1981, Box 70, Station G, Toronto.

Cvetkovich, G., & Grote, B. *Adolescent development and teenage fertility*. Paper presented at the Planned Parenthood Regional Conference on Adolescents, Boise, Idaho, June 1977.

D'Augelli, J., & Cross, H. "Relationship of sex guilt and moral reasoning to premarital sex in college women and in couples." *Journal of Consulting and Clinical Psychology*, 1975, 43, 40-47.

Dank, B.M. "Coming out in the gay world." *Psychiatry*, 1971, 34, 180-197.

DeLamater, J., & MacCorquodale, P. *Premarital sexuality*. Wisconsin: The University of Wisconsin Press, 1979.

Dryfoos, J.G., & Belmont, L. *The intellectual and behavioural status of children born to adolescent mothers*. Final report of Research of Consequences of Adolescent Pregnancy and Childbearing, National Institute of Child Health and Human Development, Washington, November, 1979.

Dunbar, J., Brown, M., & Amoroso, D.M. "Some" correlates of attitudes toward homosexuality." *Journal of Social Psychology*, 1973, 89, 271-279.

Eder, J.M. *Sexual response and genital herpes virus infections*. Paper presented at the annual meeting of the Society for the Scientific Study of Sex, San Francisco, October, 1982.

Ellis, A. *Sex and the single man*. New York: Dell Publishing, 1963.

Evans, J., Selstad, G., & Welcher, W. "Teenagers: Fertility control behavior and attitudes before and after abortion, childbearing or negative pregnancy tests." *Family Planning Perspectives*, 1976, 8(4), 192-200.

Eysenck, H.J. *Sex and personality*. Austin, Texas: University of Austin Press, 1976.

Fallon, C. *A study of adolescent mothers*. Unpublished manuscript, University of British Columbia School of Social Work, 1978.

Frappier, J. *Evaluation of a sex education program in high school*. Unpublished manuscript, University of Montreal, Montreal, Quebec, 1983.

Freeman, E.W., & Rickels, K. "Adolescent contraceptive use: Current status of practice and research." *Journal of Obstetrics and Gynecology*, 1979, 53(3), 388-394.

Furstenberg, F.F. *Unplanned parenthood: The social consequences of teenage parenthood*. New York: Free Press, 1976.

Gadpaille, W.J. *The cycles of sex*. New York: Scribner's, 1975.

Gold, D., Berger, C., & Andres, D. *The abortion choice: Psychological determinants and consequences*. Unpublished manuscript, Concordia University, Montreal, 1979.

Greenglass, E.R. *After abortion*. Toronto: Longman Canada Limited, 1976.

Guilleband, J. "Pelvic inflammatory disease and IUCDs." *British Journal of Family Planning*, 1978, 4, 25.

Guyatt, D. *Adolescent pregnancy: A study of pregnant teenagers in a suburban community in Ontario*. Unpublished D.S.W. Thesis, University of Toronto, Toronto, Ontario, 1976.

Guyatt, D. Paper presented to the Workshop on Children Raising Children, Conference of the Ontario Association of Children's Aid Societies, Toronto, April, 1981.

Hacker, S. *The effect of situational and interactional aspects of sexual encounters on premarital contraceptive behavior*. Unpublished manuscript, University of Michigan, School of Public Health, Ann Arbor, Michigan, 1976.

Hamilton, E. *Sex, with love*. Boston, Mass.: Beacon Press, 1978.

Harris, R.W.C., Brinton, L.A., Cowdell, R.H., Skegg, D.C.G., Smith, P.G., Vessey, M.P., & Doll, R. "Characteristics of Women with Dysplasia or Carcinoma in Situ of the Cervix Uteri." *British Journal of Cancer*, 1980, 42, 359.

Hass, A. *Teenage sexuality*. New York: Macmillan Publishing Co., Inc., 1979.

Hatcher, R.A., Stewart, G.K., Stewart, F., Guest, F., Josephs, N., & Dale, J. *Contraceptive technology 1982-1983*. New York: Irvington Publishers, Inc., 11th edition, 1982.

Hatcher, R.A., Stewart, G.K., Stewart, F., Guest, F., Schwartz, D. W., & Jones, S.A. *Contraceptive technology 1980-1981*. New York: Irvington Publishers, Inc., 10th edition, 1980.

Herold, E.S., Kopf, K.E., & de Carlo, M. "Family life education: Student perspectives." *Canadian Journal of Public Health*, 1974, 65, 365-368.

Herold, E.S. "The production and use of an attitudinal film in birth control education." *The Journal of School Health*, 1978, 48, 307-310.

Herold, E.S., & Thomas, R.E. "Sexual and contraceptive attitudes and behaviour of high school and college females." *Canadian Journal of Public Health*, 1978, 69, 311-314.

Herold, E.S., & Benson, R. "Problems of teaching sex education: A survey of Ontario schools." *The Family Coordinator*, 1979, 28, 199-204.

Herold, E.S., Mantle, D., & Zemitis, O. "The study of sexual offenses against females." *Adolescence*, 1979, 14, 65-72.

Herold, E.S., & Goodwin, M.R. "Why adolescents go to birth control clinics instead of their family physician." *Canadian Journal of Public Health*, 1979, 70, 317-320.

Herold, E.S. & Goodwin, M.R. "Comparison of younger and older adolescent females attending birth control clinics." *Canadian Family Physician*, 1980a, 26, 687-694.

Herold, E.S., & Goodwin, M.R. "Premarital sexual guilt and contraceptive use." *Family Relations*, 1980b, 30, 247-254.

Herold, E.S., & Goodwin, M.R. "Perceived side effects of oral contraceptives among adolescent girls." *Journal of the Canadian Medical Association*, 1980, 123, 1022-1026.

Herold, E.S., & Samson, L. "Differences between women who begin pill use before and after first intercourse." *Family Planning Perspectives*, 1980, 12, 304-305.

Herold, E.S. "Contraceptive embarrassment and contraceptive behavior." *Journal of Youth and Adolescence*, 1981, 10, 233-242.

Herold, E.S., & Goodwin, M.R. "Adamant virgins, potential nonvirgins and nonvirgins." *Journal of Sex Research*, 1981a, 17, 97-113.

Herold, E.S., & Goodwin, M.R. "Reasons given by female virgins for not having premarital intercourse." *The Journal of School Health*, 1981b, 51, 496-500.

Herold, E.S. "The relationship of abortion attitudes and contraceptive behaviour among young single women." *Canadian Journal of Public Health*, 1982, 73, 101-104.

Herold, E.S., & Way, L. "Oral-genital behaviour in a sample of university females." *The Journal of Sex Research*, 1983, 19, 327-338.

Hite, S. *The Hite Report*. New York: Dell Publishing Co., Inc., 1976.

Hobart, C.W. "Sexual permissiveness in young English and French Canadians." *Journal of Marriage and the Family*, 1972, 34, 292-303.

Hobart, C.W. "Reactions to premarital intercourse." In S.P. Wakil (Ed.) *Marriage, family & society: Canadian perspectives*. Toronto: Butterworth & Co., 1975.

Hobart, C.W. "Courtship process: Premarital sex." In G.N. Ramu (ed.) *Courtship, marriage and the family in Canada*. Toronto: Macmillan of Canada, 1979.

Hollander, X. *The Happy Hooker*. New York: Dell Publishing Co., Inc., 1972.

Hooker, E. "The adjustment of the male overt homosexual." *Journal of Projective Techniques*, 1957, 22, 33-54.

Hundleby, J.D. *Individual and environmental predictors and correlates of adolescent drug-related behaviour*. Unpublished report, University of Guelph, Guelph, Ontario, 1979.

Hunt, M. *Sexual behavior in the 1970's*. Chicago, Illinois: Playboy Press, 1974.

Hunter, M.E. "Applications for abortion at a community hospital." *Canadian Medical Assocation Journal*, 1974, 111, 1088-1092.

Jessor, S., & Jessor, R. "Transition from virginity to nonvirginity among youth: A social-psychological study over time." *Developmental Psychology*, 1975, 11(4), 473-484.

Kagan, J. *Sexual freedom: The medical price women are paying*. McCall's May 1980, 98-104, 164.

Keystone, J.S., Keystone, D.L., & Proctore, E.M. "Intestinal parasitic infections in homosexual men: Prevalence, symptoms and factors in transmission." *Canadian Medical Association Journal*, 1980, 120, 123, 512-514.

King, A., & Robertson, A. *Canada Health Knowledge Survey for ages 9, 12, and 15*. Queen's University, Kingston, Ontario, 1983.

Kinsey, A.C., Pomeroy, W., Martin, C.E., & Gebhard, P.H. *Sexual behavior in the human female*. Philadelphia, Pa.: W.B. Saunders Company, 1953.

Kirkendall, L.A. *Premarital intercourse and interpersonal relationships*. New York: Julian, 1961.

Kirkpatrick, C., & Kanin, E. "Male sex aggression on a university campus." *American Sociological Review*, 1957, 22, 52-58.

Kitchen, D.A. *Contraceptive attitudes and behaviour of young single males*. Unpublished Masters Thesis, University of Guelph, Guelph, Ontario, 1983.

Knox, S.R., Corey, L., Blough, H.A., & Lerner, M. "Historical findings in subjects from a high socioeconomic group who have genital infections with herpes simplex virus." *Sexually Transmitted Diseases*, 1982, January-March, 15-20.

Lane, M.E., Areco, R., & Sobrero, A. J. "Successful use of the diaphragm and jelly by a young population: Report of a clinical study." *Family Planning Perspectives*, 1976, 8(2), 81-86.

Lightman, E.S., & Schlesinger, B. *Maternity homes and single mothers: Three profiles*. Ontario Association of Children's Aid Societies Journal, 1980, January, 5-8.

Liskin, L.S. "Long-Acting Progestins—Promise and Prospects." *Population Reports*, Series K, No. 2, May, 1983.

Luker, K. *Taking chances*. Berkeley, California: University of California Press, 1975.

MacDonnell, S. *Vulnerable mothers, vulnerable children*. Halifax, Nova Scotia: Nova Scotia Department of Social Services, 1981.

MacKay, H., & Austin, C. *Single adolescent mothers in Ontario*. Ottawa: The Canadian Council on Social Development, 1983.

Macleod, M.A. *Opinion survey of the family planning and sex education needs in Prince Edward Island*. Department of Health, Prince Edward Island, 1980.

Mann, W.E. "Canadian trends in premarital behavior." *Bulletin of the Council for Social Services of the Anglican Church of Canada*, 1967, 198.

Mann, W.E. "Sex behaviour on campus." In W.E. Mann (Ed.), *Canada: A sociological profile*. Toronto: Copp Clark, 1968.

Mann, W.E. "Sex at York." In W.E. Mann (Ed.), *The underside of Toronto*. Toronto: McClelland and Stewart, 1970.

Margolis, A., Rindfuss, R., Coghlan, P., & Rochat, R. "Contraception after abortion." *Family Planning Perspectives*, 1974, 6(1), 56-60.

Marsman, J. *Mother-child communication about sex*. Unpublished Masters Thesis, University of Guelph, 1983.

Maslow, A.H. "Self-esteem and sexuality and women." *Journal of Social Psychology*, 1942, 16, 259-294.

Masters, W.H., Johnston, V.E., & Kolodny, R.C. *Human Sexuality*. Boston: Little Brown & Co., 1982.

McKenry, P.C., Walters, L.H., & Johnson, C. "Adolescent pregnancy: A review of the literature." *The Family Coordinator*, 1979, January, 17-28.

Mednick, B.R., Baker, R.L., & Sutton-Smith, B. *Teenage pregnancy and perinatal mortality*. Study supported by the National Institute of Child Health and Human Development of the Department of Health, Education and Welfare, Washington, D.C., 1979.

Meikle, S., Pearce, K.I., Peitchinis, J., & Pysh, F. *Parental reaction to contraceptive programs for teenagers*. Unpublished manuscript, Department of Psychology, University of Calgary, Calgary, Alberta, 1980.

Meikle, S., Pearce, K.I., Peitchinis, J., & Pysh, F. *An investigation into the sexual knowledge, attitudes and behaviour of teenage school students*. Unpublished manuscript, Department of Psychology, University of Calgary, Calgary, Alberta, 1981.

Merton, R.K. *Social Theory and social structure*. Glencoe, Illinois: The Free Press, 1957.

Miller, P., & Simon, W. "Adolescent sexual behaviour: Context and change." *Social Problems*, 1974, 22(1), 58-76.

Mosher, D.L. & Cross, H.J. "Sex guilt and premarital sexual experiences of college students." *Journal of Consulting and Clinical Psychology*, 1971, 36, 27-32.

Moskin, J.R. "Sweden: The contraceptive society." In A.S. Skolnick & J.H. Skolnick (Eds.), *Family in transition*. Boston: Little, Brown & Co., 1971.

Murdock, G.P. *Social structure*. New York: Free Press, 1949.

Orton, M.J., & Rosenblatt, E. *Adolescent birth planning needs: Ontario in the eighties*. Toronto, Planned Parenthood, Ontario, 1980.

Pelletier, L., & Herold, E.S. *Sexual fantasies among young single females*. Paper presented at the 6th World Congress of Sexology, Washington, D.C., May, 1983.

Peplau, L.A., Rubin, Z., & Hill, C.T. "Sexual intimacy in dating relationships." *Journal of Social Issues*, 1977, 33(2), 86-109.

Perlman, D. "Self-esteem and sexual permissiveness." *Journal of Marriage and the Family*, 1974, 36, 470-473.

Perlman, D. "The premarital sexual standards of Canadians." In K. Ishwaran (Ed.), *Marriage and divorce in Canada*. Toronto: McGraw-Hill Ryerson, 1978.

Phipps-Yonas, S. "Teenage pregnancy and motherhood: A review of the literature." *American Journal of Orthopsychiatry*, 1980, 50(3), 403-431.

Pool, J.S. & Pool, D.I. *Contraception and Health Care Among Young Canadian Women*. Carleton University, Ottawa, 1978.

Redmond, M. *Adolescent male attitudes toward parenthood*. Unpublished Masters Thesis, University of Guelph, Guelph, Ontario, 1983.

Reiss, I. *The social context of sexual permissiveness*. New York: Holt, Rinehart & Winston, Inc., 1967.

Roberts, E.J., Kline, D., & Gagnon, J. *Family Life and Sexual Learning*. Cambridge, Massachusetts: Population Education, 1978.

Robinson, R. *The attitudes and feelings of physically disabled adolescents about their sexuality*. Unpublished manuscript, Edmonton, Alberta, 1980.

Rosen, R.H., Benson, T., & Stack, J.M. "Help or hindrance: Parental impact on teenagers' resolution decisions." *Family Relations*, 1982, 31(2), 271-280.

Sacks, D., Macdonald, J.G., Schlesinger, B., & Lambert, C. *The adolescent mother and her child: A research study*. School of Social Work, University of Toronto, 1982.

Saghir, M.T., & Robins, E. *Male and female sexuality: A comprehensive investigation*. Baltimore, Maryland: Williams & Wilkins Company, 1973.

Saucier, J.F. "Adolescent health and prevention." *Canada's Mental Health*, 1979, 27, 21-22.

Scher, P.W., Emans, S.J., & Grace, E.M. "Factors associated with compliance to oral contraceptive use in an adolescent population." *Journal of Adolescent Health Care*, 1982, 3, 120-123.

Sherris, J.D., & Fox, G. "Infertility and Sexually Transmitted Disease: A Public Health Challenge." *Population Reports*, Series L, No. 4, Baltimore, Johns Hopkins University, Population Information Program, July, 1983.

Steinhoff, P. *Premarital pregnancy and the first birth*. Paper presented at the Conference on the Birth of the First Child and Family Formation, Pacific Grove, California, March 1976.

Stennett, R.G., Roberts, T.R., & West, N. *The Family Planning Unit of the Family Living Program: A Preliminary Evaluation*. Educational Research Services, The Board of Education for the City of London, Ontario, 1980.

Stratton, J.R., & Spitzer, S.P. "Sexual permissiveness and self-evaluation: A question of substance and a question of method." *Journal of Marriage and the Family*, 1967, 29, 434-441.

Swan, S.H., & Brown, W.L. "Oral Contraceptive Use, Sexual Activity and Cervical Carcinoma." *American Journal of Obstetrics and Gynecology*, 1980, 139, 52.

Tavris, C., & Sadd, S. *The Redbook Report on female sexuality*. New York: Delacorte Press, 1975.

Teevan, J.J. "Reference groups and premarital sexual behavior." *Journal of Marriage and the Family*, 1972, 34, 283-291.

Tietze, C., Bongaarts, J., & Schearer, B. "Mortality association with the control of fertility." *Family Planning Perspectives*, 1976, 8, 1, 6-14.

Vincent, M.O. *God, sex and you*. Philadelphia: J.B. Lippincott, 1971.

Waller, W. "The rating and dating complex." *American Sociological Review*, 1937, 2, 727-734.

Weis, D.L. "Affective reactions of women to their initial experience of coitus." *The Journal of Sex Research*, 1983, 19, 3, 209-237.

Weston, M. *Youth health and lifestyles*. A Report of Work in Progress submitted to Saskatchewan Health, August 1980.

Whitehurst, R. *Losing virginity: Some contemporary trends*. Unpublished manuscript, University of Windsor, Windsor, Ontario, 1972.

Yarber, W.L. "New directions in venereal disease education." *The Family Coordinator*, 1978, 27(2), 121-125.